Praise for *The*

Dr. Hamilton knows medicine. And he clearly knows Jesus the Healer. As these carefully woven devotionals reveal, he's a doctor of the soul.

—The Rev. Dr. M. Craig Barnes
President of Princeton Theological Seminary

. . .

Sometimes, the right book appears at just the right time. This is such a book. As we gradually recover from a life-threatening pandemic that has divided much of human society, Dr. Hamilton, a physician, senior executive, and person of deep faith, presents a book filled with stories of healing and hope. In this little volume, one encounters both faith and good sense. Most importantly, the reader meets anew the Great Healer, who alone offers ultimate hope for eternity.

—Gerald R. Winslow, PhD
Research Professor of Religion
Former Director of the Center for Christian Bioethics
Loma Linda University

. . .

Dr. Ted Hamilton is a physician in the truest sense of the word. He is a well-educated compassionate healer who possesses a kindness that embraces those fortunate enough to be in his presence. He is a pioneer in the field of physician wellbeing and the foundational nature of spirituality in healing. He is one of my heroes, and now he's taken the time to share his deep spirituality in this treasure of a book. In his inimitable style, the voice of a small-town doctor and wisdom of a truly great leader exudes in every page. We see into his healer's heart and experience Scripture in bite-sized ideas that exude warmth and hope and reflect the love God has for each of us. This book is a classic, and one that will have a permanent home on my bedside table. Many thanks to my dear friend for this gift to the world.

—Dianne McCallister, MD, MBA
Consulting Physician, Semper Healthcare

. . .

Dr. Hamilton has done a great job of providing concise yet powerful devotionals that will be a wonderful resource for chaplains, patients, and family members as they deal with challenging health issues. As a strong believer in the value of a wholistic approach to healthcare delivery and the healing process, I strongly recommend this book.

—Keith A. Parrott
President and CEO
AMITA Health

. . .

Dr. Hamilton sets out to guide the reader a little about health, a lot about healing, all about hope. I believe *The Healer* does it with grace integrating the whole person. Spirituality is a critical part to any mission focused on healing.

—Martin Schreiber, EdD
VP, Mission Leadership Institute
Providence St. Joseph Health

As a physician pastor, Ted Hamilton uses our physical health to deepen our understanding of spiritual health in *The Healer: Peace, Prayers, and Promises.* Bringing calm to crisis and clarity to chaos are gifts Ted Hamilton shares in this book. Ted quietly walks beside us on a journey for healing. He employs our understanding of physical and spiritual health to deepen our understanding of Jesus, the Healer. As a health professional, I am reminded daily of my limitations. *The Healer* helped me renew my understanding of Jesus for my own physical and spiritual healing.

—Herbert A. Schumm, MD
Bon Secours Mercy Health
VP, Medical Director, Education and Physician Engagement

. . .

Poignant, insightful, contemplative, deeply meaningful, and right on target! A compendium of the richest verses written by two of my favorite authors in Scripture come to life as Dr. Hamilton sets them into the context of our lives today. Suffering and death are present or loom in the future for all of us, but as I read *The Healer*, I felt a peaceful and calming presence portrayed on every page. He has brought the reality of Jesus' life and love in the past right down to the present, bringing to my consciousness the presence of Jesus at my side here and now. Without a doubt, the timeless reality of the Great Physician bringing hope despite trials and troubles and the assurance that death is not the end, will bless all who read this book or hear it shared by others.

—Roger D. Woodruff, MD
Chair, Department of Family Medicine
Loma Linda University School of Medicine

A beautiful and reflective compendium of biblical stories, integrating life, healing, hope, and the promise of wholeness from a God of love and grace. In a simple and practical way, Dr. Hamilton captures the intersection between the human experience and divine intervention, providing the reader a place for perspective, meaning, and future out of the daily challenges and opportunities that come to everyone's life.

—Orlando Jay Perez
VP, Mission and Ministry
AdventHealth

. . .

Dr. Hamilton provides a fresh look at the healing miracles of Jesus that makes them meaningful to all, particularly those who have, or are currently, suffering from ill health. The words flow easily from the author to the reader with an unexpected impact that brings hope.

—Eric Shadle
VP, Mission Integration
Centura Health

. . .

Jesus healed wounds by utilization of words. Ted Hamilton beautifully captures this method of treatment, providing a well-stocked pharmacy of language. These reflections are effective medicine, particularly in our seasons of acute suffering and pain.

—Alex Bryan, D.Min., M.Div.
Chief Mission Officer
Adventist Health

Dr. Ted Hamilton brings a refreshing resource to all who experience the many dimensions of illness. He gifts readers with the experience of a physician, remarkable insight into the healing ministry of Christ and the heart of a spiritual caregiver.

—Stephen King
VP, Mission Integration (Retired)

. . .

The Healer is a rich and remarkable companion for anyone on a healing journey toward health or peace. Dr. Hamilton's insightful and encouraging reflections illuminate God's word and deed, reminding us that we need not make this journey alone. Ted's authentic way of grappling with human struggle and the questions encountered on such a journey, gently reveals how God lovingly and passionately longs to provide comfort and healing, even when there is no cure, if we but open our heart, pray, and invite God's help in navigating our way.

—Patrick Gaughan
SVP, Chief Values Integration Officer
Centura Health

. . .

The Healer is a beautifully written prayerful and reflective resource for patients, families, and caregivers. The prayer book is a wonderful example of the centrality of spiritual health as we care for the whole person—body, mind, and spirit. Dr. Hamilton has written an incredibly powerful book that will provide comfort, faith, and hope for years to come to those facing serious illness.

—Dennis Gonzales, PhD
Senior Director, Mission Innovation & Integration

All of us are broken in some way and in need of healing. Sometimes we turn to healthcare workers for physical healing, but with the stresses and demands of their jobs, they are also in need of healing. This book connects all of us, patients and caregivers, with the one true source of healing, the One who desires for us to experience life in abundance but is also there to bring hope and strength when it doesn't.

—Jonathan Duffy
Senior Administrative Fellow, Kettering Physician Network

. . .

In *The Healer: Peace, Prayers, and Promises* we see that the word of God has the power to heal and make whole. Like Luke, the physician of Scripture, Dr. Ted Hamilton connects us to words of healing from God's Son. This book is food for the soul. Whether you only read the text of the day, the devotional, the prayer, or the entire reflection, now is the time to take a moment with God to nourish your spiritual core and heal the spirit.

—Chaplain (Colonel) Jonathan McGraw, U.S. Army (Retired)
Director, Strategic Ministry Initiatives
Army Chief of Chaplains, Pentagon

. . .

Many years ago, I learned that there is a difference between cure and healing. A cure addresses the infirmity or injury and leaves the body or mind with an absence of illness. But one can be cured and not healed. Healing is so much more than the absence of anything. Healing is the presence of a deep and transformative power that leads to wholeness, even when there is no cure. Jesus is never called the "curer," he never promises to remove all pain or disease, at least not in this life. But he does invite us to come into his presence and be healed. My brother and friend, Ted Hamilton, has opened the Word of God that we might better understand Jesus' ministry of healing. For anyone who needs to be made whole, come closer to Jesus through these reflections, and know that the Savior who loves you, desires for you to be healed. Come, and through this treasure, place yourself in the presence of Jesus, the Healer.

—Rev. Dr. Zina Jacque

Pastor for Small Groups,
Alfred Street Baptist Church, Alexandria, VA
Chaplain, American Baptist Churches, USA (2017-2021)

...

Dr. Ted Hamilton has captured the essence of Jesus and his irresistible love within these pages. As Luke suggests in his gospel, "Everyone was gripped with great wonder and awe, and they praised God, exclaiming, 'We have seen amazing things today!'" (Lk. 5:26). *The Healer* should be read by every patient everywhere.

—Carla Park

Executive Director, Wholeness and Faith Strategy, AdventHealth

...

As a Christian physician, Ted Hamilton has dedicated his adult life to the healing arts. I have known him for over fifty years, and his passion for bringing comfort and peace to the suffering, and those who care for them, comes as no surprise. The Healer takes the reader on a gentle journey that shines a calming light on the ministry of the Great Physician, Healer of all healers.

—James W. Davis, DDS, MS

NC Senator, Retired

THE
HEALER

Peace, Prayers, and Promises

Ted Hamilton, MD

ISBN Paperback: 978-1-954533-89-9

HigherLife Publishing and Marketing, LLC
 P.O. Box 623307
 Oviedo, Florida 32762
 (407) 563-4806
 www.ahigherlife.com

Ordering Information: Quantity sales: special discounts are available on quantity purchases by corporations, associations, and others. For details, contact the Sales Department at the address above.

Printed in the United States

10 9 8 7 6 5 4 3 2 1

To Jackie
Follower of the Healer
Experiencing His Peace
Sharing His Prayers
Embracing His Promises

Jesus' miracles are not just a challenge to our minds, but a promise to our hearts, that the world we all want is coming.
Timothy Keller

Contents

Foreword

Seventy years are given to us! Some even live to eighty.
But even the best years are filled with pain and
trouble; Soon they disappear and we fly away.
—Psalm 90:10

These ancient words are attributed to the prophet Moses, thought to have lived some fourteen hundred years before the time of Jesus the Healer, and about thirty-five hundred years before the writing of this book. But these somber words ring as true today as when they were first penned by Moses. Average longevity in the United States is about seventy-five years of age for men, and a few more for women.

Throughout time, we have struggled with infectious diseases and disorders of vital organs—brain, heart, lungs, liver, and kidneys. We have fought metabolic diseases, such as diabetes, and have sought remedies for cancerous tumors. We continue to experience tragic illnesses and injuries related to accidents, warfare, and the inevitable process of aging.

We need a Healer.

Certainly, modern medical science has made monumental advances in diagnosis and treatment of illness. Advanced imaging procedures, including X-rays, CT scans, and MRI, along with sophisticated blood and genetic analysis have contributed to our understanding and ability to detect disease earlier and devise more effective treatment plans. Physicians and nurses are better trained than ever before, with capabilities that Moses could never have imagined. Anesthesia, antibiotics, and advanced surgical techniques offer relief and aid recovery. But we continue to experience illness, injury, and loss.

We need a Healer.

In the pages of this book, Dr. Ted Hamilton draws from the gospel story of Jesus the Healer, and applies lessons learned to twenty-first century medical care. Regardless of the historical setting, diagnosis, or treatment regimen, illness and injury are accompanied by pain, fear, anxiety, worry, and distress. The reassuring words of the Healer, as recorded in the gospel story, continue to provide comfort, alleviate fear, reduce anxiety, instill hope, and dispel distress.

I encourage you to meet and become better acquainted with Jesus the Healer through the pages of this book and experience his love, joy, and peace in times of difficulty and distress.

Harold G. Koenig, MD
Director, Center for Spirituality, Theology and Health
Professor of Psychiatry & Behavioral Sciences
Associate Professor of Medicine
Duke University Medical Center

Preface

Health is an almost indescribably wonderful thing. But good health can be all too easily taken for granted when one feels whole—blessed with a strong body, a clear mind, and a serene spirit. The everyday story of human life, though, reveals that good health is impermanent, an all-too-frequently transient experience, to be enjoyed, celebrated with gratitude in the moment, and fervently sought after in its absence.

When health is interrupted by illness or injury, healing becomes a wonderful thing. The human body has remarkable innate healing resources, the ability to fight infection, knit broken bones, soothe bruises, stanch bleeding, cover cuts and scrapes with new skin. But sometimes the body needs the help of a healer, someone to set the broken bone, to remove the diseased appendix, to prescribe the right medication.

Sooner or later, for all who draw breath, for all of us, health runs out and healing is not forthcoming. We all face the vulnerability of health, and ultimately, the transience of life. But we are never without hope. Hope contains within itself the potential for healing, for restoration of health. Hope that acknowledges reality, however bleak, and continues to contemplate the potential, the possibility, of healing, is not false hope. It is real and it is powerful.

This book is a little about health, a lot about healing, and all about hope. It is intended for those who are experiencing illness and injury, for those who love and care for them, and for all who have an interest in learning more about the Healer who brought health, healing, and hope into our world some two thousand years ago and who continues to do so today.

Introduction

Today, almost three million people will be cared for in hospital outpatient facilities and clinics in the United States.[1] One hundred thousand patients will be admitted to hospitals for diagnosis and treatment. On any given day, over six hundred thousand patients will occupy hospital beds.[2] If you are one of these people, concerned about your health, or experiencing an illness or injury, this book is for you.

Based on the biblical story of Jesus the Healer, as applied from the perspective of a modern-day family physician, this book is intended to provide peace and hope to those seeking healing. Pondering the story of the healing ministry of Jesus helps us appreciate the dramatic capabilities of twenty-first century medical care combined with the enduring healing influence of prayer, faith, hope, and love.

This book follows the gospel narrative as recorded in the New Testament books of Luke and John. Luke, whose gospel closely parallels those of Matthew and Mark, is believed to have been a physician. The book of John provides a viewpoint in many ways unique to the gospel bearing his name. Together, Luke and John record twenty-one of the twenty-six specific healing miracles of Jesus. For the sake of completeness, Jesus' remaining five recorded healing miracles are included in this book, drawing three from Matthew and two from Mark.

To provide continuity, the story moves sequentially, back and forth between John and Luke. Every effort has been made to provide a cohesive and chronologically sound story. Although not technically a theological commentary, nor a classic devotional book, nor a straightforward narrative, but comprising aspects of each, this book is intended to be a faithful and practical application of Scripture to healing and healthcare as practiced in this country today.

Those who prefer to read this book from beginning to end, first page to last, will benefit from having a Bible close at hand to afford access to the full story. In place of a devotional title, complete scriptural references are provided at the beginning of each entry so that interested readers can locate each passage in the Bible. The specific verses that form the basis of each comment are quoted in the text following the scriptural reference and preceding the author's comment.

The twenty-six specific healing miracles of Jesus are recorded as they appear in the narrative flow and are identified with a dove symbol ❧.

A full chronological healing miracle index is also provided along with a theme index. Scriptural references to multiple, but otherwise unidentified, healing miracles are listed following the reference to Luke 7:24–33. Scriptural references are from the familiar New Living Translation (NLT) unless otherwise noted.

LIFE & LIGHT

Life and Light echo throughout
John's narrative.

Luke 1:1–4
The Storytellers

John 1:1–18
Beginning at the Beginning

Luke 1:5–80
*Two Unexpected Pregnancies and
Two Songs of Thanksgiving*

Luke 2
Birth & Childhood of the Healer

Luke 3 & John 1:19–51
The Baptizer & The Chosen One

• Luke 1:1–4 •

*Many people have set out to write accounts about
the events that have been fulfilled among us. They
used the eyewitness reports circulating among us
from the early disciples. Having carefully investigated
everything from the beginning, I also have decided to
write an accurate account for you … so you can be
certain of the truth of everything you were taught.*

. . .

This is a story, a very old story, of a Healer who walked the
earth some two thousand years ago. Born in poverty and
obscurity, in a small backwater province of the Roman empire,
he would grow up to become an itinerant preacher, teacher, and
healer whose life and teachings would forever change the world.
This story is told from the perspective of Luke, a physician, and
John, one of the closest followers and most devoted disciples of
the Healer. His words and deeds continue to encourage, to comfort, and bring hope and healing to those who hear his story
and experience his grace today. The name of this Healer is one
of the most familiar in all the world—Jesus. His story begins at
the beginning of it all.

*Blessed Healer, I come to you to experience your
love and care. May I, too, become a gift of healing
to those who touch my life today.*

• John 1:1–5 •

In the beginning was the Word.... The Word was
God.... His life brought light to everyone. (vv. 1, 4)

. . .

In the beginning.
   In the beginning of the cosmos and of our world, in my beginning and your beginning, he was. He was our Creator, and he is our God.

He gave us life and he brings us light, light that cannot be extinguished.

This light, his light, shines in our darkest night and through our deepest despair, dispelling the shadows, defeating the darkness, and illuminating the path ahead.

Lord God, Maker of the cosmos, Creator of all that is, Light-Bearer, Life-Giver, Healer, be all to me today, and make of me a vessel of your light, life, love, and healing to all whose lives I touch.

4

• John 1:6–13 •

*To all who believed him and accepted him, he gave the
right to become children of God.* (v. 12)

. . .

Really? Does it mean what it says? It sounds too good to be
true.

How marvelous, how intriguing, how inviting to become
a child again—to see color with new eyes, to hear music with
new ears, to first savor the taste of vanilla ice cream, to touch a
kitten's fur with new fingers, to experience anew the warmth of
a mother's embrace.

*Life-Giving Lord, let me become that child—
born again into innocence and possibility,
peace and promise, hope, and a future bright
with love and joy.*

• John 1:14–18 •

*So the Word became human and made his home
among us.* (v. 14)

. . .

The Creator-God who made my world, and gave me body, breath, and soul, has come to live with me and share my journey. He knows. He knows me, all about me—all my pain, my regrets, my worries, my fears—and he loves me anyway. When I am at my best, the Word of Life is cheering me on. When I'm at my worst, he's picking me up. Whether I'm weak or strong, wise or foolish, confident or desperate, his unfailing love and faithfulness sustain me.

Lord God, Maker of all who live and all that is, remember me today as I struggle with illness, pain, doubt, and worry. Give me assurance of your presence and peace.

• Luke 1:5–7 •

*[They] were righteous in God's eyes.... [but] they had
no children because Elizabeth was unable to conceive,
and they were both very old.* (vv. 6–7)

. . .

You know the desire of our hearts is to have a baby, a child to love and nurture. How can it just happen—so easily, even accidentally—for our friends, and not for us? What is wrong with us? How can we be left out of the joy of conception, the anticipation of childbirth, the fulfillment of a baby in our arms? We're good people. We love each other. We can support a family. Why does the cradle remain empty?

*O Lord of life, Creator, Healer,
hear our prayer and complete our
love with life.*

• Luke 1:8–17 •

God has heard your prayer. Your wife, Elizabeth, will
give you a son … John. (v. 13)

. . .

It's not every day that an angel shows up on the job site with a message meant for you. Just going about your business, the same old routine, nothing out of the ordinary—and an angel calls your name—your very name. That'll get your attention for sure. And the angel's message? Unbelievable! Your elderly wife who is long past the age of reproduction is going to have a baby, a special baby (aren't they all?), who will become a great man by the grace and purpose of God. Name him John, the angel says. Just common, ordinary John. This John's life, though, will be anything but common and ordinary.

Lord God of all, I'm just an ordinary person.
I'm not the smartest or strongest and
certainly not the most beautiful or handsome.
But I want to be your servant. May your will be
done in my life today.

• Luke 1:18–22 •

You will be silent and unable to speak until the child
is born. (v. 20)

• • •

Speechless. Have you ever been struck speechless? Don't know what to say? No words! Dumbstruck! Sometimes the best response is mere silence. Sometimes the only possible response is to remain mute. Sometimes silence is the body's response to surprise or shock. Sometimes silence is the most comforting thing that can be said.

O God who spoke the world into existence, give me the grace to be silent in the presence of the holy, to withhold speech in moments of deep understanding, to hold the precious moment in silent awe.

• Luke 1:23–25 •

*Soon afterward, Elizabeth became pregnant…. "How
kind the Lord is!" she exclaimed. (vv. 24–25)*

. . .

How could I have suspected it? How could I have known? I
thought it was a sign that my body's ability to conceive was
gone for good. And then, then I felt a little thump in my tummy
… then another … and then a third. And I knew … I knew … I
knew it was true. My dream had come true; a baby was growing
inside me! Oh delight! Oh joy beyond expression!

---

*Kind Lord, I'm not a person who prays out loud
in public where others can hear. But my heart is
too full. I cannot hold back. I must tell you. I must
say thank you. Thank you for your kindness, your
goodness, and your grace. Thank you for hearing
and answering my prayer. Thank you for taking
away my shame, my loneliness, my grief. Thank
you for giving me new life and hope and joy.*

• Luke 1:26–29 •

*[The angel] Gabriel ... appeared to her [Mary] and
said, "Greetings, favored woman!" (v. 28)*

. . .

Favored? Really? Why me? I'm only a girl, becoming a woman, and engaged to be married. Why would this strange, angelic being suddenly appear to me? Is this real? Am I dreaming? Or am I feverish and ill? How can I describe this experience? Who will listen? Who will believe me? Who will care? "The Lord is with you," he says.

Lord God, be with me today. May I perceive your presence. Speak to me. Help me understand and accept whatever comes my way today with you at my side.

• Luke 1:30–38 •

*You will conceive and give birth to a son, and you
will name him Jesus.* (v. 31)

. . .

How can this be happening to me? Oh, I know it's happened
countless times before and will happen countless times to
come—conception before wedlock, and no earthly man willing
to share responsibility for the act, the outcome, the child. How
can I tell my parents? How can I shame my betrothed, and what
will he say? Worse, what will he do? How can I visit the local
market? People will avert their eyes and turn their backs. How
can I go to church wearing maternity garments? Nevertheless,
let it be as the angel has said.

---

*Unfailing God, be with me and with the new life
I carry within my body—my baby. Give me the
strength and courage, the confidence and hope,
the knowledge and common sense to do my best,
hold my head up, and walk a straight path.*

• Luke 1:39–45 •

*At the sound of Mary's greeting, Elizabeth's child
leaped within her. (v. 41)*

. . .

Two women (distant cousins), two unanticipated pregnancies, two baby boys in utero (cousins yet more distant). Instant recognition, immediate understanding, unquestioning compassion, shared joy.

Thank you, Lord, for aunts and uncles and cousins when times are tough.

Thank you, Lord, for Granny and Gramps who have a spare bedroom and an extra chair at the table.

Thank you, Lord, for the neighbor lady three doors down on the left who has "been there, done that," and who understands my heart.

---

*Thank you, Lord, for being a God I
can trust to do what you say
you will do.*

• Luke 1:46–56 •

Mary responded, "Oh, how my soul praises the Lord.
How my Spirit rejoices in God my Savior!"
(vv. 46–47)

. . .

Sometimes mere prose, however eloquent, is inadequate to express the heart's throb. Sometimes the moment requires and inspires the gift of poetic expression. There may seem to the untrained ear, the untuned mind, no particular rhyme nor reason, but the heart, the heart hears, and feels, and knows.

Praise God.
Praise God from whom all blessings flow.
Praise God for caring for generations of
the humble and needy.
Praise God for feeding the hungry,
clothing the naked, and sheltering the homeless.
Praise God for his power, his mercy,
his grace, and his love.
Praise God.

• Luke 1:57–80 •

But Elizabeth said, "No! His name is John!" (v. 60)

. . .

Everyone showed up for the big reveal. Neighbors, relatives, and closest friends came to celebrate the naming of the newborn child, just eight days old. The guests thought he should be named after his father, Zechariah. But his mother would have none of it. She was adamant, "No! His name is John." And Zechariah attested to the same in writing. It seems to have worked out okay. Some two thousand years later, people still talk about their son, John. And his name remains one of the most popular for baby boys born in the United States today.[3] The hand of the Lord was on little John and the hand of the Lord is on little girls and boys like John today.

To the Name above all names, cause me today to honor the name I carry. May I be true to the heritage, the integrity, the aspirations, and the love it reflects.

• Luke 2:1–20 •

She [Mary] gave birth to her firstborn son. She wrapped him snugly in strips of cloth and laid him in a manger. (v. 7)

. . .

No wonder she went into labor when she did. She was a strong young woman, used to hard work and walking long distances, but a week-long hike of ninety miles at nine months gestation over rough terrain—what were they thinking? Maybe Mary hitched a ride on a donkey part of the way. Either way, this baby was due to deliver.

Some say he was born in a stable and others say it was in a shallow cave that housed livestock and their keepers on cool nights. In any case, it was a meager, humble shelter with a feeding trough for a cradle. In attendance, an adoring woman, a devoted man, and a healthy baby with a few astonished shepherd guests and an angel choir singing praise to God and proclaiming peace on earth. Every new baby should be so fortunate.

Lord God, attend the birth of this baby. Bless our baby, and every baby born today, with life and breath and strength. Teach us to sing with the angels, "Glory to God in highest heaven, and peace on earth" (Luke 2:14).

• Luke 2:21–40 •

Simeon ... took the child in his arms and praised God.... Anna, a prophet, was also there ... and she began praising God. (vv. 28, 36, 38)

. . .

Old people get it.

They may have cataracts, astigmatism, and glaucoma, but their vision is twenty-twenty.

They may have to use canes, walkers, or wheelchairs, but they get around.

They may use hearing aids and memory devices, but they know stuff.

Simeon and Anna were very old, but they knew at first sight that the baby was someone special. First they told his parents; then they told everyone who would listen that great and terrible things were in store for him. And they were right.

Old people get it.

Great God of young and old, be with me in all of life—its spring, summer, fall, and winter. Make me faithful and give me true voice that I may share your blessing with fidelity and grace.

• Luke 2:41–52 •

Jesus grew in wisdom and in stature and in favor with God and all the people. (v. 52)

. . .

It's not just one thing or another. It's all of it packaged together—growth into wholeness of mind, body, spirit, and community. To concentrate on one at the expense of the other is to risk compromise of all. To develop all within one's natural gifts and abilities is to enrich the whole.

Dear Lord, we thank you for this growing child you have given us to raise, to nurture, to love. We thank you for the inexpressible joy this life brings us. We pray now for wisdom, grace, patience, and foresight to raise our child to be like Jesus, growing daily in every way— physically, mentally, spiritually, and socially.

• Luke 3:1–6 •

Isaiah had spoken of John when he said, "He is a voice shouting in the wilderness, 'Prepare the way for the Lord's coming!'" (v. 4)

. . .

Sometimes my life just seems to be a never-ending series of detours and dead-ends, obstacles and potholes, storms, and squalls. Just when it appears that the skies are clearing and things are getting better, it clouds over and the road heads down toward another disaster. Illness, broken promises, job loss, and disappointments, one upon another, seem to be my lot in life.

Dear Lord, open my eyes and show me your way. Clear my path. Give me the courage to put my trust in you, that I might experience your love and accept your healing grace in my life.

• Luke 3:7–14 •

The crowds asked, "What should we do?" (v. 10)

...

It's not rocket science. It's not glorious deeds and amazing feats of prowess. It's not self-punishment, guilt, worry, and fear. That's not what a good and proper life is about; that's not what God asks. It's rather simple really. It's not hard to understand, though it's not always easy to do, not our natural human inclination. Be kind. Share with those who are poor and hungry. Be honest. Do the right thing. Show mercy. Forgive. Be gentle. Be humble. Treat others as we wish to be treated. Love one another.

Eternal Guide, be with me on life's journey today.
Teach me what to say and how to say it;
what to do and how to do it; where to
show up and how to appear with kindness;
how to follow you and share your love with
those whom I meet along the way.

• Luke 3:15–20 •

John used many such warnings as he announced the
Good News to the people. (v. 18)

…

"Do you swear to tell the truth, the whole truth, and nothing but the truth, so help you God?"

"I do."

But then I don't. At best, I tell my version of the truth. The truth as I saw it, experienced it, perceived it. At worst, I fabricate, color, distort, or create an alternate version to serve my own ends. After all, truth is dangerous. Truth is painful. Truth causes trouble. Truth also clarifies, cleanses, heals, and restores. Albeit through pain and tears, truth is worth the telling.

All-Knowing God, help me this day to hear
and comprehend the truth. I fear. The truth
may be painful. It may be frightening.
It may be intimidating, discouraging,
depressing. I relinquish my fear to you
and accept your faithfulness in its place.

• Luke 3:21–22 •

*And a voice from heaven said, "You are my dearly
loved Son, and you bring me great joy." (v. 22)*

. . .

What remarkable words! Amazing to say. Incredible to
hear. "You are my dearly loved [child], and you bring
me great joy." Gracious words. Life-giving words. Affirming
words. Comforting words. Encouraging words. Healing words.
Words to be held in the heart and treasured always. Today is the
perfect day to hear those words—and to say them to your child.

---

*Loving Lord, may your gracious words ring in my
ears all this day long. May I hear you say, "dearly
loved" and "great joy" over and over. May these
words become such a part of me that I find myself
repeating them once and again to my family, my
friends, and my caregivers.*

• Luke 3:23–38 •

Jesus was known as the son of Joseph. (v. 23)

. . .

I've neither studied my ancestry nor had my DNA tested. I'm only familiar with the last two or three generations of my family tree. But I know that, in my family, we've had soldiers and sailors, loggers and car dealers, beauties and brawlers, doctors, nurses, and teachers. Some of us were conceived within, and some out of, wedlock. We've suffered heart disease, cancer, mental illness, miscarriage, alcoholism, and suicide. We've experienced some good fortune and a lot of misfortune. We've argued and fought and kissed and made up (almost always). In other words, our family is pretty much like yours. And if we follow our family trees, yours and mine, back to the beginning, the very beginning, we learn that we're all God's children, imperfect at best, but accepted and loved despite our flaws and failings.

God of all, in whose image we all are made, from whom we have received the gift of life, and in whom we find our greatest contentment and joy, make us grateful. And in gratitude, teach us to love one another.

• John 1:19–28 •

John replied in the words of the prophet Isaiah: "I am a voice shouting in the wilderness, 'Clear the way for the Lord's coming!'" (v. 23)

. . .

Who are you?

Sometimes it's easier to answer that question with a "not." I'm not a world class athlete. I'm not a Rhodes scholar. I'm not a star of stage or screen. I'm not a wealthy business tycoon. I'm not a mover and shaker, nor a trendsetter.

Well then, who are you?

Sometimes it's easier to answer that question with a "just." I'm just a schoolteacher. I'm just a security guard. I'm just a trash collector. I'm just a waitress at the local deli. I'm just a bus driver. I'm just a baggage handler.

Who are you, really?

Perhaps you are a person who prepares the way, who plans next steps, who manages details, who works behind the scenes, largely unnoticed, but a person without whom the event would never happen, without whom people would not be fed, without whom the report would be inaccurate or delayed, a person important, essential even, a person who offers strength and support for the benefit of others.

Lord of the least and of the most and all those in between, fulfill my life by making of me everything you would have me be.

• John 1:29–34 •

I [John] saw this happen to Jesus, so I testify that he is the Chosen One of God. (v. 34)

. . .

It's sometimes a good thing to be chosen—chosen for the basketball team, chosen for the homecoming court, chosen for a promotion, chosen as a friend.

Sometimes it's not so good to be chosen—to get stuck with the tab, to clean up after the party, to muck out the horse stall, to deliver the bad news.

Sometimes it's a heavy responsibility to be chosen—to balance the books, to perform the wedding, to raise the children, to count the votes.

To be chosen by God for a special purpose—to be a faithful spouse, a responsible parent, a loving child, a trusted friend—may somehow be reflective of all the above, depending upon circumstances and challenges, but always, and ultimately, for good when one is chosen by God.

---

*Good God, what is your choice for me today?
Show me your will and your way. Give me the
wisdom to discern, the will to follow,
and the strength to do that which you have
chosen for me to do.*

• John 1:35–51 •

"Nazareth!" exclaimed Nathanael. "Can anything good come from Nazareth?" (v. 46)

. . .

Can anything good come out of your hometown? That's what was asked about the place where Jesus was raised. Where were you born and raised?

- Wisconsin has a Great Lakes shoreline and famous cheese.
- Illinois claims generations of colorful politicians, including Abe Lincoln.
- Kansas provides fertile ground for amber waves of grain, especially wheat.
- Colorado is home to over fifty mountain peaks exceeding fourteen thousand feet elevation.
- Texas is big enough for fields of bluebonnets and pastures of Longhorn cattle.
- Georgia soil nurtures fruit and nuts—peaches, pecans, peanuts.
- Kentucky racehorses feed on justly famous, high octane, bluegrass.
- North Carolina is bookended by the Atlantic barrier islands and Smoky Mountains.
- Florida beaches and theme parks host holiday guests from around the world.
- Where were you born and raised? Can anything good come from there?
- Well, for starters, there's you. And those you love. And the history that formed you. And the future that awaits you.

Father God, your Son, Jesus, the best of good men, came from the poor, disrespected town of Nazareth. By your grace, make me a bearer of good things from my humble place of origin.

PEACE IN THE STORM

Peace weaves a continuous thread
through Luke 4–9.

John 2, 3
For Better or Worse God Loves You

John 4, 5, 6
Food and Water; Life and Death

Luke 4, 5
Good News and Going Home

Luke 6, 7, and Matthew 9
The Touch of the Healer

Luke 8, 9
The Healer and the Sixth Sense

• John 2:1–12 •

The next day there was a wedding celebration.... This miraculous sign at Cana in Galilee was the first time Jesus revealed his glory. (vv. 1, 11)

. . .

"Do you take this person to be your lawfully wedded spouse, to have and to hold, for better or worse, for richer or poorer, in sickness and in health, as long as you both shall live?"

"I do."

"I do."

So let the celebration begin! Welcome the guests. Bring out the food and the drink. Let the music begin.

Sing. Dance. Feast. Laugh.

Lord, bless these lovers ... this union ... this new beginning ... this new family ... this new home. May it be a refuge of peace, love, and joy.

• John 2:13–25 •

He [Jesus] told them, "Get these things out of here.
Stop turning my Father's house into a marketplace!"
(v. 16)

. . .

Spring Cleaning.
Wash the windows.
Beat the carpets.
Polish the floors.
Clean out the closet.
Organize the garage.
Store the blankets.
Pull back the shades.
Open the windows.
Oil the hinges.
Have a yard sale.
Enjoy a picnic.
Turn the tables.
Spring is here.

Father, there's a lot of clutter in my life—dust,
cobwebs, smudges on the windows, scratches on
the floor, squeaky hinges, stuff out of place.
Give me the courage to take out the trash,
straighten the furniture, clean the windows,
and make room for you.

• John 3:1–9 •

Jesus replied, "I tell you the truth, unless you are born again, you cannot see the Kingdom of God." (v. 3)

. . .

Ten thousand babies will be born in the United States today.[4] Without a conscious thought, without a plan, without instructions, ten thousand babies will take a first breath, see a mother's face, feel a mother's touch, take nourishment, sense a mother's love. It all just comes naturally to a newborn baby.

How many people will be "born again" today?

Are you kidding me? What are you talking about?

It's a strange thought. Some would say it's incomprehensible, nonsense, bizarre. How can this be? Perhaps it's not so out of the ordinary or complex as it seems. Perhaps it simply means to take a deep breath, see the world with new eyes, feel the stirring of a new spirit within the heart, find nourishment for the human soul, and experience the love of our Creator God.

Dear Lord, let me see life today through the eyes of a newborn baby.

• John 3:10–15 •

*And as Moses lifted up the bronze snake on a pole in
the wilderness, so the Son of Man must be lifted up, so
that everyone who believes in him will have
eternal life.* (vv. 14–15)

. . .

The Caduceus.

It's a strange symbol, really—a live serpent (or two)
wrapped around a pole or a cross. The caduceus can be seen
on doctor's offices, clinics, hospitals; as a logo on medical
equipment, uniforms, and supplies; in medical journals,
advertisements, and promotional materials. Some attribute the
two-serpent caduceus to Greek or Roman mythology. The one-
serpent motif is referenced in the Old Testament, or Hebrew
Bible, as a symbol of life and protection from the ravages of a
poisonous serpent infestation. According to the scriptural story,
those who looked upon the uplifted serpent were healed.

---

*Dear Lord, may we look to you today for health,
healing, and hope.*

• John 3:16–21 •

For this is how God loved the world: He gave his one
and only Son, so that everyone who believes in him
will not perish but have eternal life. (v. 16)

. . .

Arguably the most widely known and best loved words of Scripture, John 3:16 ranks right up there with the Lord's Prayer (Luke 11), the Shepherd's Psalm (Psalm 23), the Beatitudes (Matthew 5), and the Golden Rule (Matthew 7). Perhaps that's why we see it on placards at major sporting events, displayed on church signs and public billboards, and even printed on garments.

- God loves us, all of us, all the world around.
- God loves us, all of us, so very much.
- God loves us, all of us, and gave his Son to live his love among us.
- God loves us, all of us, and invites us to believe that he is love.
- God loves us, all of us, and wants to be with us, living forever.
- God loves us, each and every one of us, fully, unconditionally, eternally.

Lord God, thank you for your love, for the gift
of your Son, for life eternal.

• John 3:22–26 •

So John's disciples came to him and said, "Rabbi ...
the one you identified as the Messiah, is also baptizing
people. And everybody is going to him instead of
coming to us." (v. 26)

. . .

There are almost eight billion people living in the world today.

There are over two billion who identify as Christian believers.

There are about one-and-a-half-billion adherents of the Islamic faith.

There are about one billion who observe Hinduism.

Another billion claim no religion, identifying as secular, atheist, agnostic, or none.

There are about a half-billion Buddhists worldwide.[5]

Of professed Christian believers, about half are Catholic and a third are Protestant. It is estimated that there are thousands of separate and distinct organized Protestant faith groups. There seems to be a natural inclination for Christian people to disagree over doctrine or practice or worship style or music or whatever, leading to separation and division.

Loving Lord, may we learn to love you and to
truly love each other, forgiving each other as we
have been forgiven.

• John 3:27–36 •

John replied, "No one can receive anything unless
God gives it from heaven." (v. 27)

. . .

I have a friend who is an amazing musician, a classically-trained pianist who also plays beautifully by ear. I have another friend who is an artist, a painter who has the ability to translate her vision to paper with remarkable clarity and beauty. I have a friend who possesses an innate ability to understand complex financial concepts and convert seemingly obtuse fiscal facts in a simple and straightforward, understandable manner. I am not a musician, an artist, or a financial whiz.

Creator God, teach me to accept who I am and
make the most of your unique gifts to me.
And may I fully appreciate and applaud the
richness that my talented friends bring
into my life.

• John 4:1–15 •

Soon a Samaritan woman came to draw water, and
Jesus said to her, "Please give me a drink." (v. 7)

. . .

Please give me a drink of water.

Have you ever been thirsty? Really thirsty? So thirsty that
your tongue feels like cotton? Mouth so dry that you can hardly
swallow? So dehydrated that you feel light-headed and weak?
Lips chapped and skin parched? Headache and nausea?

Please give me a drink of water.

Just a cup of fresh, clear, cool water. Or, if necessary, an
intravenous solution comprised of water and essential nutrients,
sugar, and salt, to fill the bloodstream, nourish the vital organs,
and help the body recover sufficiently to tolerate fluids taken by
mouth.

Please give me a drink of water.

Can you imagine drinking a cup of water from a deep well,
or a clear spring, or just from the refrigerator that would so
relieve your thirst that you would never become thirsty again?
That's what Jesus offered the woman whom he met at the well
near Sychar. You can't blame her for misunderstanding his offer.
The water he offered was not what she had intended to draw
from the well, but water drawn deeper yet—water to refresh
and restore a tired, dry, parched soul.

Dear Lord, please give me a drink of water.
Refresh my body and restore my soul today.

• John 4:16–26 •

The woman said, "I know the Messiah is coming—the one who is called Christ. When he comes, he will explain everything to us." Then Jesus told her, "I AM the Messiah!" (vv. 25–26)

. . .

We wear masks. Halloween masks and masquerade balls turn us into ghosts and goblins, heroes and movie stars, famous athletes, and cultural icons. We wear masks for health and safety reasons—to protect others from coughs and sneezes, to avoid transmission of bacteria and viruses. We wear masks to protect ourselves from noxious fumes and chemicals. And sometimes we wear masks to protect us from ourselves—when we want to see ourselves, and be seen by others, as something (or someone) different from whom we know ourselves to be.

Having astonished and unmasked the Samaritan woman by demonstrating his knowledge of her past, Jesus removed his own mask and revealed his identity: "I AM the Messiah" whom you seek. And that changed her life for good.

Lord God of all, help me to remove my mask, to show my face, to reveal my heart, to be the person you would have me be—genuine, authentic, real.

• John 4:27–38 •

*But Jesus replied, "I have a kind of food you know
nothing about." (v. 32)*

. . .

I'm not hungry anymore.

That's what he said. It hardly makes sense. He hadn't eaten
a bite.

It would make more sense if he were under great stress,
or perhaps consumed with a compelling task. Under difficult
circumstances, sometimes one's appetite just seems to
disappear. But, he said, I have food—food that might seem
strange to you. My food, my nourishment, comes from doing
what I came among you for—to do the will of God. Jesus was
fed and nourished by meeting and making a difference in the
life of a young woman searching for answers, for truth. That was
nourishment sufficient to the moment.

---

*Provider God, fill me with that for which you
know I hunger, and may I be fully satisfied with
your all-knowing provision.*

• John 4:39–42 •

"Now we believe, not just because of what you told us, but because we have heard him ourselves. Now we know that he is indeed the Savior of the world." (v. 42)

. . .

There are different ways to learn.

Some people learn best by reading a book or manual. Others learn best by paying attention in the classroom.

Some learn best by seeing, others by hearing, and still others by doing.

Some things are learned from others; some things you must learn for yourself.

And sometimes it's a combination of these that opens the mind and heart. As it did for the Samaritan villagers who heard the woman's story and then met the teacher. Who heard his voice, watched his work, and believed. "Now we know," they said, "that he is indeed the Savior of the world."

Dear Lord, to be with you is to know you; to know you is to love you, and to love you is to trust you. Teach me today to know you better, to love you more, and to trust you always.

• John 4:43–54 •

The official pleaded, "Lord, please come now before my little boy dies." Then Jesus told him, "Go back home. Your son will live!" (vv. 49–50)

. . .

He had heard about Jesus. Perhaps he had heard the miracle story about the wine at the wedding in nearby Cana and surmised that if Jesus could do that, maybe Jesus could help his sick child. When he learned that Jesus had returned to his part of the country, he set out to find him.

Most every parent who ever lived resonates with this story. Never a child escapes childhood untouched by illness or injury. Rare indeed is the parent who would not gladly bear pain and distress in place of their child, and rarer yet the parent who would not explore every avenue and pay any price to find a source of help and healing for their little one.

This is the first of twenty-six specific healing miracles of Jesus recorded in the gospels. Jesus told the man, "Your son will live." And the child lived.

Healing Lord, watch over my child today. Ease the pain, relieve the suffering, revive the spirit, restore the laughter, return the joy of life and health.

• John 5:1–15 •

One of the men lying there had been sick for thirty-eight years. When Jesus saw him and knew he had been ill for a long time, he asked him, "Would you like to get well?" (vv. 5–6)

. . .

Who wouldn't like to get well?

Who wouldn't want to experience healing?

Who wouldn't want to feel "just like my old self?"

Who wouldn't want to be whole?

Who wouldn't want to walk in the park again after an amputation?

Who wouldn't want to wake up in the morning without arthritic pain?

Who wouldn't want to hear, "Your cancer is in remission"?

Who wouldn't want to be whole?

Who wouldn't rejoice to see the "blue dot" after fertility treatment?

Who wouldn't be joyful to go a full month without a migraine?

Who wouldn't celebrate on leaving the ICU after heart surgery?

Who wouldn't want to be whole?

Who wouldn't marvel at a sunset after an eye injury?

Who wouldn't celebrate their baby's graduation from the NICU?

Who wouldn't want to hug a friend after isolation for infection?

Who wouldn't want to be whole?

Dear Lord, I pray today for the experience of wholeness. Despite my difficulties, regardless of my current situation, give me, I pray, a sense of your presence and your love for me.

• John 5:16–30 •

"Indeed, the time is coming when all the dead in their graves will hear the voice of God's Son, and they will rise again." (vv. 28–29)

. . .

There's something about a cemetery that I like, that draws me.

Maybe it's the quiet that's conducive to reflection, meditation, prayer.

Maybe it's the pastoral beauty, mowed lawns, colorful flowers, majestic trees.

Maybe it's the sense of history, of people and ages past, of days done and gone.

Maybe it's the seeming presence of those I love, those whose bodies rest there—grandparents, aunts and uncles, Mom and Dad.

There's something about a cemetery that I hate, that repels me.

Maybe it's the sound of sadness and grief—wailing, sobbing, silence.

Maybe it's the freshly turned dirt, wilted flowers, unruly weeds here and there.

Maybe it's a sense of the future, of the relentless passage of generations to come.

Maybe it's the absence of those I love, and the imminent passing of my cousins, my siblings, my spouse, me.

Dear Lord, God of life eternal, I am encouraged and comforted today by your promise,

"The time is coming when all the dead in their graves will hear the voice of God's Son, and they will rise again."

May that time be soon.

• John 5:31–47 •

*"You search the Scriptures because you think they
give you eternal life. But the Scriptures point to me!"*
(v. 39)

. . .

Finger pointing seems to have gotten a bad name. Often a
pointed finger accompanies a verbal accusation or a threat.
Loud voices, unkind words, frightful body language and facial
expressions.

But the words of Jesus above point a different direction,
redeeming the pointed finger. "The Scriptures," he said, "point
to me." That would have been the Hebrew Bible to which he
referred, the ancient books that comprise the Old Testament—
the accounts of God's mighty acts in history, the lyrical songs
of David, the pithy wisdom of Solomon, the stories of valor and
faith of men and women of old, and the prophecies concerning
a child who would become the Messiah, the Christ, the Healer
and Redeemer of the world. That's me, he said.

---

*Healing God, take away the pointed fingers
of my past. Point me toward a future of
security and hope.*

• John 6:1–15 •

Turning to Philip, he [Jesus] asked, "Where can we find bread to feed all these people?" (v. 5)

. . .

Hunger is part of the experience of being human. We are born to experience hunger. Every day we awaken to a sense of hunger, and we begin each new day with a breaking of our overnight fast, our breakfast, only to experience a recurring sensation of emptiness as the day passes, prompting a search for food to assuage our hunger.

Jesus knew hunger, too, and he recognized it in others. On more than one occasion, he demonstrated his catering ability by providing food for great crowds of people. His method was simple—take what is at hand, little or much, pray over it, giving thanks to God, and share it with everyone.

Some call it a miracle; some say that the words and actions of Jesus prompted everyone to share what they had. What is known is that it was more than enough for everyone. More than enough to fill empty stomachs and starving souls.

Dear Bread-Maker Lord, give us this day our daily sustenance, and open our hearts and hands to share your gracious bounty so that all who are hungry may be fed.

• John 6:16–21 •

But he [Jesus] called out to them,
"Don't be afraid. I am here!" (v. 20)

. . .

A hospital room can be a very lonely place. Day or night, when one is confined and ill and visitation is limited, the sense (or reality) of isolation, of aloneness, can be discouraging, frightening, even depressing.

To the ill and bedridden, Jesus says, "Don't be afraid. I am here."

In the reassuring voice of the doctor, Jesus is here.

In the tender touch of the nurse, Jesus is here.

In the prayer of the pastor or chaplain, Jesus is here.

In the broom and mop of the housekeeper, Jesus is here.

In the strong arms and legs of the transporter, Jesus is here.

In the thoughtful preparation of nourishment and meals, Jesus is here.

And in the quiet of an otherwise empty room, Jesus is here.

Comforter Lord, let me feel the security of
your presence just now.

• John 6:22–59 •

*Jesus replied, "I am the bread of life. Whoever comes
to me will never be hungry again. Whoever believes in
me will never be thirsty." (v. 35)*

. . .

Sometimes an illness is of such a nature and severity that
the body cannot tolerate food and water that are consumed
in a normal manner. Swallowing is difficult and painful; the
stomach rejects whatever is presented to it, or the bowels may
be inflamed and swollen or blocked. In these circumstances,
it is necessary to provide nourishment in another manner,
thereby bypassing or alleviating the problem and allowing the
body to heal. This may require nutrients to be provided by a
tube placed in the stomach or even introduced directly into the
bloodstream through intravenous fluids.

Jesus assures the hungry and the thirsty that he is the bread
of life; he is the living water, and that everyone who believes in
him has eternal life.

---

*Dear Lord, provider of all good things, fill me,
nourish me, refresh me, keep me in your love.*

• John 6:60–70 •

At this point many of his disciples turned away and deserted him. (v. 66)

. . .

"Fair weather friends," they're called. Here today, gone tomorrow. Here for the good times, for the fun and games, the picnics and parties, the weddings and birthdays. Gone when trouble looms, when the economy tanks, when the diagnosis is grim.

Jesus understands that too. Scripture says that many of his closest followers walked away, failed to show up the next morning, deserted him without so much as a goodbye. That's one of life's most crushing, devastating experiences.

And then there are those who stay. Like the disciple Simon Peter, who knew of no other person who could offer words that give eternal life.

Dear Lord, we believe. Help us to stick with you through thick and thin.

• Luke 4:1–13 •

Then Jesus … was led by the Spirit in the wilderness,
where he was tempted by the devil for forty days. Jesus
ate nothing all that time and became very hungry.
(vv. 1–2)

...

I'm tempted.

When my tray is late, the hot food is cold, and the ice cream is melted, I'm tempted to send it back untouched. When my surgery is scheduled for nine-thirty in the morning and the transport team doesn't come for me until two-forty-five in the afternoon, I'm tempted to blame the doctors, the nurses, and the hospital. When my hospital bill makes no sense at all, and I can't find anyone to explain it, I'm tempted to shred it and trash it.

When my family doesn't visit my hospital room, I'm tempted to disown them. Well … not really, but that's how I feel sometimes.

When Jesus was hungry, poor, and unknown, he was tempted with food, wealth, and fame. He confronted the Tempter with truth, trust, and fidelity.

And the Tempter left him. Perhaps Jesus' response will work for me too.

Overcoming Lord, I pray that you will lead me away from temptation, deliver me from the evil one, and continually strengthen my trust in you.

• Luke 4:14–21 •

*He [Jesus] went as usual to the synagogue on the
Sabbath and stood up to read the Scriptures.* (v. 16)

. . .

Are you feeling down and out? Are you at the end of your
rope?

Is it hard to see the next turn in the road, much less envision
a healthy future?

Does it seem like you'll never recover and return to normal?

Do you feel trapped by circumstances beyond your control?

What would you give to hear some good news? A bit of hope
for the future?

Listen to Jesus' healing words, drawing from the Hebrew
prophet Isaiah.

His message to you in these verses is clearly, "I have
good news, good news for the poor, the out-of-luck, the
downhearted. I bring keys to open long-locked doors, offering
fresh air and freedom to captives."

---

*Healing Lord, remove the scales from my eyes
and restore my vision and my hope. I gladly claim
the promise of a new day ... the day of the Lord's
favor has come to me.*

• Luke 4:22–30 •

Everyone spoke well of him and was amazed by the
gracious words that came from his lips. "How can this
be?" they asked. "Isn't this Joseph's son?" (v. 22)

. . .

Going home is a mixed bag.

Whether the absence has been six months or sixty years, there seems to come a bittersweet nostalgia, a longing for the good old days combined with a feeling that things are different, that the life one once knew in that place and time can never be the same.

The homeplace is smaller than you recall. The trees have grown so that the house is partly hidden from the street. The backyard, no longer cluttered with croquet wickets, bicycles, sandbox, and ping pong table, now features garden plots for flowers and vegetables.

The neighbors, except for a few, have moved away and those who remain are older, slower, grayer. But they remember you, your games, your pranks, your accidents, and childhood accolades.

Going home is a mixed bag.

Companion Lord, you know all about us. You know where we've been, what we've done, and who we are today. The little, skinned-knee, runny-nosed kids that we once were remain alive in our memories, and we still need you in our lives today.

• Luke 4:31–37 •

Amazed, the people exclaimed, "What authority and power this man's words possess! Even evil spirits obey him, and they flee at his command!" (v. 36)

...

Amazed, the people exclaimed, "What authority and power this man's words possess! Even evil spirits obey him, and they flee at his command!" (v. 36)

- Replacing a heart valve without making an incision in the chest—amazing.
- Transplanting bone morrow as part of cancer treatment—amazing
- Walking without pain on a pair of brand-new knees—amazing.
- Performing delicate surgery on a baby still in the womb—amazing.
- Restoring sight by replacing cataract-clouded lenses with clear ones—amazing.
- Enjoying mental health through a carefully crafted medication regime—amazing.

The privilege of extending the healing ministry of Christ—amazing.

Healing Lord, thank you for demonstrating your power over illness, injury, and pain. Thank you for your amazing grace.

• Luke 4:38–44 •

*No matter what their diseases were, the touch of his
hand healed every one.* (vv. 40–41)

. . .

Sometimes it makes the evening news—an auto accident
with multiple injuries, an illness befalling a famous, wealthy,
or influential person, a Nobel prizewinning breakthrough
in medical technology. But most of the time, it just happens
without notice or fanfare—no headlines, no fireworks, no
parade down Main Street. Just common, everyday illness
and injury—sore throat, runny nose, fever, sprained ankle,
headache, joint pain, nausea, itchy rash, cuts, bumps, and
bruises. They're assessed, treated, and comforted, and most of
the time, they get better.

Jesus was an "equal opportunity" Healer. He gave each
patient individual, personalized attention. Whether it was
Simon's mother-in-law, "very sick with a high fever," or one of
the many unnamed village people who came to him for help,
Luke (a physician) records that "no matter what their diseases
were, the touch of his hand healed every one." The touch of
Jesus' hand still heals today.

*Dear Lord, bless me that I might experience the
touch of your healing hand today.*

• Luke 5:1–11 •

Jesus replied to Simon, "Don't be afraid! From now on you'll be fishing for people!" (v. 10)

...

I f it sounds sorta fishy, that's because it's a fish story.
Not a big, bigger, biggest fish ever caught story.

Not a story about the big one that got away.

Not a big fish in a little pond story. Nor a little fish in a big pond story.

It's a story about a long, frustrating night on the lake with no luck at all.

The fish just weren't anywhere to be found. The nets were empty. The fishermen were tired. They pulled in the nets and rowed toward shore.

And then a man standing on shore said, "Try again."

Against their better judgment, against all fishing odds, they did. And the fish filled the nets to breaking. Then the man on the shore said, "Follow me. We have bigger fish to fry." So they did. They left their nets and followed him.

And that's no fish story.

---

*Good Lord, help me to hear you when you call.
Give me the good sense to follow your advice and
to go wherever you lead.*

• Luke 5:12–16 •

"Lord," he [a leper] said, "if you are willing, you can
heal me and make me clean." (v. 12)

• • •

Let's face it, "dirty" is often a dirty word. The word "dirty" has multiple associations, some good and some not so good.

We expect the hands of farmers and gardeners to reveal contact with the soil.

The clothing of painters is often splashed and splattered at the end of the day.

Oil, grease, and grime are the mediums in which machinists and mechanics work. But "dirty" is not so good a word when it is linked to suspicion, complicity, or active involvement in misbehavior.

Hospitals, clinics, and surgery centers are required to be more than clean. Procedures involving the human body are required to be both clean and sterile, not just free of "dirty" substances, but cleansed of microscopic organisms that might cause infection. For patients, families, doctors, nurses, in fact, for everybody, the single most important method of managing "dirty," preventing infection, and protecting each other is frequent and thorough handwashing, something that we all can do.

Lord of Order and Beauty, bless those who clean clinics and hospitals today. Bless those who carefully wash and sterilize surgical instruments. Bless the soap-and-water washed hands of our caregivers. Give me clean hands and a pure heart.

• Luke 5:17–26 •

Some men came carrying a paralyzed man on a
sleeping mat.... Then they lowered the sick man on his
mat down into the crowd, right in front of Jesus.
(vv. 18–19)

. . .

Friends. What a blessing! What a comfort! What security! What a joy to have friends, real friends, caring friends. It's been said, "a friend in need is a friend indeed."

Do you have someone who loves and cares for you? A friend who will stand up, show up, and speak up for you? Someone who calls to check on you from time to time? Someone who stops by to make sure you're okay? Someone to pick up your medications, who will help you get to your doctor's appointment on time, who will tell you the truth? A friend who will laugh at your jokes, listen to your worries, and hold your hand when you're in distress? A friend who will pray with you and for you? Do you have a friend?

Dear Lord, thank you for my friends. Thank you
for their words of encouragement, for their gifts of
love and caring, for their presence in my life when
times are tough.

• Luke 5:27–32 •

Jesus answered them, "Healthy people don't need a doctor—sick people do." (v. 31)

. . .

How do you know when you need a doctor?

- When the pain is really bad and getting worse.
- When the sore just won't heal.
- When the lump keeps on growing.
- When the bone is broken, or the heart.
- When you're always thirsty for no good reason.
- When you're losing weight with no apparent cause.
- When the fever is unrelenting, or persistent nausea and vomiting.
- When your spouse says you must, or the paramedic.
- When something is not right, but you can't say why.
- When you know you should, but you've been putting it off.
- When it's clear that simple home remedies and homespun advice don't help.

And the list goes on …

"Healthy people don't need a doctor—sick people do." That's what Jesus said.

Forgiving Lord, help me not to deny or ignore my symptoms. Let no false pride keep me from making an appointment with my doctor. Hold me up as I submit to examination and testing. I place my trust in you.

• Luke 5:33–39 •

Then Jesus gave them this illustration: "No one tears a piece of cloth from a new garment and uses it to patch an old garment." (v. 36)

. . .

Make sure the patch is a proper match.

I don't think that's an old proverb, but perhaps it should be.

It's certainly good advice for organ transplant surgeons.

It's one of the many miracles of modern medicine that permits the transplantation of essential organs from one person to another, from a compatible donor to a needy recipient, affording improved function and prolonging life. Hearts, lungs, livers, and kidneys, carefully matched to prevent rejection by the recipient immune system, provide new life.

Lord of Life and Creation, thank you for medical and surgical expertise of those who perform these miracles daily. Thank you for kind, generous, selfless organ donors, who, in life and in passing, provide new patches for old, worn-out organs. Thank you for new life today and eternal life to come.

• Luke 6:1–11 •

Then Jesus said to his critics, "I have a question for you. Does the law permit good deeds on the Sabbath, or ... is this a day to save life or to destroy it?" (v. 9)

. . .

What's good and what's bad? Who decides? How are these decisions made? And how are these decisions enforced?

Good and bad, bad and good, these are important, fundamental questions that are critical to the functioning of every society and every culture. Everyone has an opinion, and everyone, sooner or later, is impacted by cultural allowances and prohibitions. Life and experience, religion and politics, custom and habit, education and debate form our opinions and practices of right and wrong.

Is it okay to do good? Is it okay to relieve pain, to heal the sick and injured, to save life? These questions of Jesus go straight to the heart of our humanity. When, if ever, is it inappropriate or unacceptable to relieve suffering? His answer was to relieve and restore and heal anytime, all the time, whenever and wherever there was a need. That's the right answer yesterday, today, and tomorrow.

Dear Healer and Restorer, thank you for your healing grace, offered freely and timely to all, given without barriers, boundaries, or restrictions.

• Luke 6:12–16 •

One day soon afterward Jesus went up on a mountain
to pray, and he prayed to God all night. At daybreak
he called together all of his disciples and chose twelve
of them to be apostles. (vv. 12–13)

. . .

He chose twelve. And a motley crew they were. Several fishermen, a right-wing patriot and a left-wing liberal collaborator, a cynic, a doubter, and a thief. Two brothers were known as "sons of thunder." (I don't know why, but I'm pretty sure it had nothing to do with the daily weather.) Jesus spent three years with the twelve, traveling from place to place throughout Palestine, teaching, preaching, and healing. And sharing lessons of life—kingdom life, he called it, kingdom life in a common, everyday world. He encouraged them, chastised them, trained them, and sent them out on their own to follow his example. He sent them out to do as they had observed him do, visit the towns and villages—teach, preach, and heal. And along the way, they began to understand, albeit slowly and dimly, what he was all about. They continued to have their differences; they continued to question, debate, disagree, argue, and compete for position among themselves. But he never gave up on them.

Thank you, Lord Jesus, for never, ever giving up on
me, regardless of my religion, politics, or behavior.
Catholic, Protestant, Muslim, Buddhist, Hebrew,
or "None." Democrat, Republican, or Independent.
Man, woman, or child. Cynic, doubter, or thief.

• Luke 6:17–19 •

Everyone tried to touch him, because healing power went out from him, and he healed everyone. (v. 19)

...

He healed everyone.

When you come to the Emergency Department for your illness or injury, we will take care of you. No matter who you are, where you are from, or what your concern is, we will take care of you. Whether you have commercial insurance, Medicare or Medicaid, or no insurance at all, we will take care of you. Whether you are a native-born United States citizen, a recent immigrant (legal or not), or a foreign visitor, we will take care of you. Heart attack or headache, stubbed toe or stomachache, sore throat or stroke, dizziness or depression, numbness or nausea, we will take care of you. Regardless of age, gender, nationality, or presenting complaint, we will take care of you.

That's our job, our promise, our mission. We will take care of you.

Lord God, thank you for quality healthcare. Thank you for sophisticated medical technology and procedures. Thank you for dedicated, professional caregivers. Remind me to express my appreciation to those who care for me today and every day.

• Luke 6:20–26 •

*What blessings await you when people hate you
and exclude you and mock you and curse you as
evil because you follow the Son of Man. When that
happens, be happy! Yes, leap for joy! For a great
reward awaits you in heaven. (vv. 22–23)*

. . .

Upside down, inside out, sense and nonsense.

Are you poor, hungry, sad, or lonely? Jesus says you are blessed.

Are you rich, popular, full of food and laughter? Jesus says beware.

Upside down blessings. Inside out sorrows. Sense or nonsense?

The world we know, the world we live in, often appears upside down.

What we see on the outside is often at odds with what exists on the inside.

I don't get it. It doesn't seem right or proper or fair. It just doesn't make sense.

---

*God of the upside-down kingdom, give me
patience and courage and strength to face today's
challenges and bear today's burdens. Give me
humility and gratitude and generosity to share
today's gifts and blessings. Give me insight and
wisdom and faith to trust your will and
your way for my life.*

• Luke 6:27–36 •

*"I [Jesus] say, love your enemies! Do good to those
who hate you. Bless those who curse you. Pray for
those who hurt you.... Do to others as you would like
them to do to you." (vv. 27–28, 31)*

. . .

Here's what I like.

I like sunshine, rainstorms, and rainbows.

I like Greek food, Thai food, Mexican food, Indian food, and Italian food.

I like walking in the mountains, by the seashore, around the neighborhood.

I like reading good books, history, biography, adventure, mystery.

I like hot chocolate, cool lemonade, fresh squeezed orange juice, and cold water.

I like family and friends and holidays and good times together.

I like marriages, births, graduations, and meaningful, rewarding work.

---

*Dear Lord of all, give unto others all those things
that make me happy and be especially gracious to
all those with whom I disagree. Enable me to do
for others as I wish that others do for me.*

• Luke 6:37–42 •

*Then Jesus gave the following illustration: "Can one
blind person lead another? Won't they both fall
into a ditch?" (v. 39)*

. . .

It's time for my twice-yearly checkup with the eye doctor. I
am a challenging eye patient. I have myopia (hard to see at a
distance) and hyperopia (need glasses for reading). I also have
glaucoma (elevated eye pressure) for which I use drops every
day, and dry eyes, for which I apply gel every night. I also have
pesky "floaters" in my left eye that require the periodic attention
of a retinal specialist. And I also have had cataracts in both eyes
(a recent surgery was successful).

But, thank God, I can still see—to read, drive, write a note,
watch my grandchildren grow up. But I don't take my eyesight
for granted, and my heart goes out to those who have vision
challenges.

*Dear Lord of light, give me a heart of gratitude for
eyes that see. Shed your healing grace
on those who struggle to see. Thank you for
good doctors, effective medicine, and
modern surgical techniques.*

• Luke 6:43–49 •

"What you say flows from what is in your heart."
(v. 45)

. . .

The fountain in the back yard is simple and inexpensive. About three feet high and about fifteen inches around, it is colored in random shades of gray. A twelve-gallon water basin is hidden beneath the fountain and, when activated by a timer switch, the pump inside the basin pushes water up through a slender hose to emerge in a gentle stream, filling the shallow fountain and cascading down its sides to be recaptured in the basin to continue circulating until the timer reaches "Off."

The simple beauty of the fountain and the soothing sound of the water create peaceful memories.

But following a storm, the fountain can be inundated with falling leaves, twigs, sand, dirt and debris. The water may be discolored or even disabling to the pump. It becomes necessary to turn off the electricity, turn the fountain on its side, and clean out the basin, removing the trash and replacing murky water with fresh, clean water.

Dear Lord, cleanse my heart, I pray. Make me a clear-flowing fountain, sharing clean, calming, refreshing water from a heart filled with peace.

• Luke 7:1–10 •

At that time the highly valued slave of a Roman officer
was sick and near death.... And when [they] returned
to his house, they found the slave completely healed.
(vv. 2, 10)

. . .

Here's the situation.

He is a working man in a service industry. Works hard, doesn't complain, takes home a check that allows his family to get by. They make it, barely, until he gets sick and can't go to work. It's a hard time.

His supervisor is a good and kind man, fully aware of the circumstances. He urges a visiting doctor to make a house call on the sick man. The doctor agrees, and, upon examination, determines that Dad needs to be in the hospital.

I don't recall the details, but I do recall my dad's illness, and I remember the doctor who made the house call. I seem to recall that it took a day or two for Dad to fully recover, but he was soon on his feet and back to work.

It's a challenge to measure the healing effect of prayer or to determine the direct source of healing. But I know this, I know my dad was prayed for, and I know he recovered, and I know that he had a good boss and a good doctor, and our family is forever grateful.

Healing God, thank you for hearing our prayers
and thank you for answering in ways beyond our
understanding.

• Matthew 9:27–34 •

Two blind men followed along behind him, shouting,
"Son of David, have mercy on us!... Then their eyes
were opened, and they could see!... "Nothing like this
has ever happened in Israel!" they exclaimed.
(vv. 27, 30, 32)

. . .

Two men, both blind, both believing, both healed.
Two men, sternly warned to keep it quiet.

But who can blame them for putting up billboards all over Israel, for posting on Facebook and Instagram, for agreeing to interviews on the evening news?

Who can blame them? They can see! They can see! No surgery, no glasses, no contacts, no medication! They can see! And they want everyone to know.

They were barely out the door before a man thought to be demon-possessed presented with inability to talk. Before he walked out, the demon had disappeared, and the man spoke. The man was ecstatic; the crowd was amazed, but some folks grumpily suggested that the devil was behind it all from the get-go.

Dear Lord, Healer of all those who
believe, Lord of all who seek you: May I seek and
trust you. May I see with my eyes and speak with
my tongue of what you have done for me.

• Luke 7:11–17 •

Then he [Jesus] walked over to the coffin and touched it, and the bearers stopped. "Young man," he said, "I tell you, get up." Then the dead boy sat up and began to talk! And Jesus gave him back to his mother.
(vv. 14–15)

. . .

I've been witness to the deaths of many people. As a family physician, I was well acquainted with most of those who breathed their last under my care. They succumbed to the usual severe, acute, and chronic diseases that are responsible for most deaths in this country—heart disease, cancer, lung disease, diabetes mellitus, accidents. For most, death was tragic, but not unexpected, the result of genetics, old age, and/or poor health habits—years of smoking, lack of exercise, dietary indiscretion, and risky behaviors, not infrequently related to substance dependence and abuse.

I have yet to witness a resurrection, a return to life after being pronounced dead. Oh, I've participated in cardiopulmonary resuscitation, with varied results. Most died, but a few responded to these emergency measures and lived to tell the story. So, it is possible. It can happen, but a full recovery is infrequent, if not extremely rare.

But when resurrection fails to happen right in front of our eyes, that does not mean the end for those who trust the Healer who has promised a home where sadness and tears are no more and life is eternal. This heaven is the expectation of those who hope, who believe.

Dear Life-Giving Lord, I place myself and my future in your hands, for good or ill, secure in the knowledge that you love and care for me and will walk with me through the valley.

• Luke 7:18–23 •

*Then he [Jesus] told John's disciples, "Go back to John
and tell him what you have seen and heard—the blind
see, the lame walk, those with leprosy are cured, the
deaf hear, the dead are raised to life, and the Good
News is being preached to the poor." (v. 22)*

...

Are you the one … the real deal … the one we've been expecting?

How does one answer that question? It's so broad and all-encompassing. You want to get it right. Jesus' answer went straight to the heart of it.

Jesus said to watch and take notes then to go back to John and tell him what you've seen. Pretty comprehensive and concise. Incontrovertible evidence. Just watch and be convinced. The Gospels record twenty-six specific healing miracles of Jesus, and while those healings attracted attention, the Gospels attest to a broader, wider healing ministry, touching hundreds, if not thousands, of lives of people who came to him for help.

Perhaps your recovery wasn't unique, dramatic, or spectacular, but it is a miracle nevertheless. It's your miracle. Your healing. Outside of your family and close friends, perhaps no one knew or noticed. Few knew of your illness, your pain, your worry. But Jesus the Healer knew, and he cared, and he heard your prayers and answered. The medications worked. The treatments provided comfort. The surgeon removed the tumor. Jesus healed your body.

*Jesus the Healer, thank you for hearing my
prayers, for caring for me, for healing me.*

Countless Miracles

Additional, numberless healing miracles of Jesus for unidentified people throughout his ministry and travels.

- Matthew 4:23: "Throughout ... Galilee ... he healed every kind of sickness and disease."
- Matthew 9:35: Wherever he went, "he healed people of every kind of disease and illness."
- Matthew 12:15: "Many people followed him. He healed all the sick among them."
- Matthew 14:14, 35–36: A vast crowd was there. "He had compassion on them and healed their sick.... All who touched him were healed."
- Matthew 15:30–31: "He healed them all.... And they praised the God of Israel."
- Mark 1:32–34:"Jesus healed many people who were sick with various diseases."
- John 6:2: "A huge crowd kept following him wherever he went, because they saw his miraculous signs as he healed the sick."

• Luke 7:24–35 •

Wisdom is shown to be right by the lives
of those who follow it. (v. 35)

. . .

The proof is in the pudding.

It's not enough to talk the talk. You must walk the walk.

As we think in the heart, so we become.

And wisdom is proven credible and valid in the lives of those who follow it.

Smart is not necessarily wise. Nor is clever, canny, or wily. Good grades, a great job, or immense popularity don't guarantee wisdom. Sometimes it is necessary to pass through pain, disappointment, and failure on the hard and rocky road to wisdom.

All-Wise Lord, touch me by your grace, give me of your wisdom, bless me with understanding and thanksgiving.

• Luke 7:36–50 •

*Then Jesus said to the woman, "Your sins are
forgiven…. Your faith has saved you; go in peace."*
(vv. 48, 50)

...

No wonder the good people, the connected, the influential,
the law-abiding citizens viewed Jesus with suspicion. It
wasn't that he was a bad person or that he scoffed at their laws.
It had a lot to do with his friends, the people with whom he
hung out. They called him a glutton and a drunkard, a friend of
tax collectors and sinners. And he didn't deny it.

We're not told whether she had a record, but she certainly
had a reputation. She was well-known and apparently well-
compensated. And it was at a dinner for Jesus and his friends
that she chose to openly demonstrate her love for him. The host
pretended to be appalled, but Jesus called him out, provoking
him to undermine his own critique. And then he said to the
woman, "Your sins are forgiven…. Your faith has saved you; go
in peace."

---

*Dear Lord Jesus, friend and companion of sinners,
trusted restorer of the rejected and the outcast.
Be for me, today, the ultimate source of
forgiveness and peace.*

• Luke 8:1–15 •

When they look, they won't really see. When they
hear, they won't understand. (v. 10)

. . .

When is the last time you recall looking straight at something, but not seeing it?

When have you heard a familiar tune and couldn't recall the song a minute later?

John Claypool, a well-known pastor and teacher, was fond of repeating the truism:

What vision is to beauty,

And hearing is to melody,

What smell is to fragrance,

And taste is to flavor,

What touch is to texture,

So is faith to spiritual experience.[6]

Faith is the eyes, ears, nose, mouth, and skin through which we see, hear, smell, taste, and touch the transcendent, the deeply inner knowing, the sixth sense, through which we come to love and trust God.

Dear Lord, thank you for the gift of my senses—
sight, smell, hearing, taste, and touch. Give me an
appreciation for the beauty, melody, fragrance,
flavor, and texture that surround me. And give me
faith to trust your will and way for my life.

• Luke 8:16–21 •

Jesus replied, "My mother and my brothers are all those who hear God's word and obey it." (v. 21)

. . .

Who is your family?

On its surface, it seems an easy question. My family is Dad and Mom, my siblings and me. That's true, but it's not the whole truth. How about grandparents, aunts and uncles, and cousins? And how about my new little cousins who were recently adopted from a country far away? Or how about Uncle John, who was married to my mother's sister before she died? Is he still family? When divorce and remarriage complicate the picture, who is family? Is family all, none, or some yes and some no? Who decides?

And then there's my school family, teachers, coaches, classmates, and friends. The truth is, I feel closer to some of them than to my "real" family. We work together, eat together, play together, and hang out together.

And don't forget my work family, my church family, and my club family, and … well, you get the idea. The answer to the question, "Who is your family?" depends on the people involved. It depends on the history, the setting, and the circumstances, but most of all on the relationships we have with each other.

Jesus understood the complexity of this question, when he said in Luke 8:21, "My mother and my brothers are all those who hear God's word and obey it." He was not neglecting his mother, whom he deeply loved, nor was he ignoring his birth brothers, whom he cared for as well. But he was clearly making a point—family is who we choose to be our family. Family is the people we care for and who care for us. Family transcends blood and birthright to incorporate those to whom we are attached by bonds of love and loyalty.

Dear Lord Jesus, thank you for my family and bless us today, each and every one of us. Despite our mistakes, missteps, and failures, help us to love each other, appreciate each other, and care for each other. Help us to understand and empathize with each other, putting our arms around each other, holding each other up.

• Luke 8:22–25 •

*When Jesus woke up, he rebuked the wind and
the raging waves. Suddenly the wind stopped and
all was calm. (v. 24)*

. . .

Perhaps you've been in a storm, not simply a summer
thunderstorm with lightning, thunder, wind, and rain that
is dramatic but short and mostly harmless. Nor winter's first
snowfall, with big, fluffy white flakes falling softly to cover grass
and shrubs, only to melt and run off by mid-morning. Neither
the thunderstorm nor the snowfall would make the evening
news.

Maybe you're facing a storm right now, a storm that
threatens your health, your livelihood, your future. Perhaps
your diagnosis is not yet clear, or your doctors are undecided
about your course of treatment. Or maybe you're facing surgery
and the prognosis is uncertain.

Maybe you're blinded by the lightning, deafened by the
thunder, unsure of your course? Scripture says that Jesus
rebuked the wind and calmed the waves, the storm stopped,
and all was peace.

---

*Dear Lord, master of wind and waves, calm the
storm in my soul today and give me peace.*

• Luke 8:26–39 •

Jesus demanded, "What is your name?"
"Legion," [many] he replied.... The man who had been
freed from the demons ... was sitting at Jesus' feet,
fully clothed and perfectly sane." (vv. 30, 35)

. . .

Mental illness.
Substance dependence.
Homelessness.
Incarceration.

Four distinct problems, but somehow connected. Not necessarily cause and effect, but there is a clear association among them. A high percentage (many) of our homeless population suffer from mental illness and/or substance dependence. This often contributes to behaviors that lead to incarceration. Our correctional institutions are often ill-prepared to deal with the complex physical, mental, social, and spiritual issues that characterize the lives of those who present with various combinations of these conditions.

As a nation, as communities, as caregivers, as concerned citizens, as family and friends of people facing these challenging circumstances, we must lean in. We must love those who have few to love them. We must care for those who have few to care. We must pray for the grace of God to touch their lives.

Do you find yourself in such a place today? Don't give up. Don't try to go it alone. Don't go back to the same old places, with the same old crowd, doing the same old things that brought you here. Reach out, seek support, accept help, pray for God's blessing.

After healing the man called Legion (many), Jesus said, "Go

back to your family, and tell them everything God has done for you" (Luke 8:39).

Lord Jesus, Healer, today I pray the best I know how. Heal me, body, mind, and soul. Make me new. Make me clean. Restore me to my family. Give me life.

• Luke 8:40–56 •

"Daughter," he [Jesus] said to her, "your faith has made you well. Go in peace." (v. 48)

...

These two stories cannot be separated; they are intertwined. Disease and death do not discriminate; they do not acknowledge priorities, do not respect rank, position, or authority, and play no favorites.

A twelve-year-old girl was dying. An older woman was troubled with a chronic disease of twelve years duration. Unable to address both problems immediately, a decision must be made. Who will get the Healer's attention first? Who must wait? What are the implications of this decision?

Accidents with multiple injuries, mass battlefield casualties, and pandemics which overwhelm medical staff and clinical resources may require healthcare professionals to make these kinds of crisis decisions. Covid-19 has raised similar questions, such as who should be prioritized for limited testing availability, who should receive limited, life-saving medications, and who should be first to receive the vaccine when it becomes available. These questions pose serious moral and ethical dilemmas for governing bodies and for society at large.

The older woman took matters into her own hands, literally touching Jesus' garment as he passed by, she experienced immediate healing. Word came back that the little girl had died in the meantime, but Jesus, undeterred, made a house call to her home and restored her to life and health. Jesus remains today the Healer of all, regardless of age, gender, status, ethnicity, or condition.

Lord Jesus, Healer, allow me to touch your garment today. Hear my cry. Hear my prayer. Bless the doctors and nurses who care for all who hurt and suffer. Give them wisdom and courage and compassion. Thank you for hearing and answering prayer.

• Luke 9:1–6 •

*Then he [Jesus] sent them out to tell everyone about
the kingdom of God and to heal the sick.* (v. 2)

. . .

Perhaps your hospital is a "teaching hospital," meaning a
hospital where medical students and residents are trained in
preparation for taking their place as fully equipped practicing
physicians.

Medical students come to your bedside following the
completion of a full year of basic science, including human
anatomy and physiology, biochemistry, microbiology,
embryology, and genetics. A second year is devoted to
the clinical sciences, including neurosciences, cardiology,
pulmonology, gastroenterology, and other major body systems,
and what happens when things go wrong (pathology). They
arrive in the hospital in the third and fourth years of medical
training, to learn about you, and to learn from you, and, in
learning, to help you.

Residents are graduates of medical school, continuing their
training in various specialties, such as Internal Medicine,
Surgery, Obstetrics & Gynecology, Pediatrics, Emergency
Medicine, Family Medicine, and related subspecialties.
Residency training may last from three to seven years,
depending on the specialty. Residents learn from experienced
physicians, fully trained specialists in their various fields.
Residents supervise and teach the medical students under their
supervision, and residents take care of us in the process of
mastering their specialties.

Like the disciples of Jesus, medical students and residents
are "sent out" to care for ill and injured people in clinics and

hospitals. Under the direction of senior physicians, they diagnose diseases, prescribe treatments, comfort patients, communicate with loved ones, and prepare for full-time independent practice.

Dear Lord and Teacher, please bless the medical students and residents who will care for me today. Give them clear thinking, wise judgment, practiced hands, and the ability and humility to care for me and others with love, kindness, and skill.

• Luke 9:7–17 •

Jesus took the five loaves and two fish, looked up toward heaven, and blessed them.... They all ate as much as they wanted. (vv. 16–17)

...

Chances are you're just feeling so poorly that you don't have much of an appetite. Or maybe you've been placed "NPO" and cannot have any nourishment by mouth. Or maybe your stomach does not welcome anything you have eaten but threatens to send it right back where it came from. Or maybe hospital food just doesn't taste like your favorite home cooking. In any case, food has become unavailable or unappealing to you.

Dear Lord, you who made all good things for us to eat, I pray for relief from pain and nausea. I pray for recovery and healing and the return of a healthy appetite.

• Luke 9:18–36 •

*"The Son of Man must suffer many terrible things," he
[Jesus] said.... "He will be killed, but on the third day
he will be raised from the dead." (v. 22)*

. . .

Predicting the time of one's demise is not a good idea. It
is a foretelling fraught with imprecision and error. "They
give him six weeks to live," or "She's not likely to make it past
her anniversary," or "He's not expected to leave the hospital."
This sort of prediction can be wrong either direction. He may
pull together his strength and last months longer on grit and
determination. She may experience an unexpected complication
that draws down her last remaining energy and strength.

What do we say? What do we do in these difficult and
sensitive circumstances? Regardless of the timeliness of the
prediction, it's a good time to settle matters, not just business
and financial matters, but personal and family issues.

- It's a good time to say, "I'm sorry."
- It's a good time to say, "Please forgive me."
- It's a good time to say, "I forgive you."
- It's a good time to say, "Thank you."
- It's a good time to say, "I love you."

Simple words. Familiar words. Sometimes hard to say.
Always worth saying. Especially when the end, albeit uncertain,
appears inevitable.

---

*Dear Lord of all comfort, give me the words to say,
the courage to say them now, and the love to say
them in a way that heals wounds and gives peace.*

• Luke 9:37–43 and Mark 9:22–27 •

The father said to Jesus, "Have mercy on us and help us, if you can." "What do you mean, 'If I can'?" Jesus asked. "Anything is possible if a person believes." The father instantly cried out, "I do believe, but help me overcome my unbelief!" … Jesus took him by the hand and helped him to his feet, and he stood up.
(Mark 9:22–24, 27)

Jesus rebuked the evil spirit and healed the boy. Then he gave him back to his father. (Luke 9:42)

. . .

You just feel so helpless. You've done everything you know to do. If only you could take this trial on yourself instead of watching your child deal with the pain and misery and uncertainty of her condition. You've taken her to many physicians, tried many medications and treatments. She's undergone invasive tests and multiple surgeries. The symptoms resist resolution. The illness changes and morphs, always seeming one step ahead of your best efforts.

When disappointment follows disappointment, it's sometimes hard to keep going, to keep trying, to continue making an effort, to sustain hope for a better future. In times like these, we pray with the father of the sick boy, help my unbelief.

Dear Lord of all mercy, take what little faith I have and multiply it. Make it real and living and powerful. Relieve my child's pain, restore his health, give back his strength and his hope. Praying with all the faith I can muster, with all the faith within me, I put my fervent prayer before you.

• Luke 9:44–62 •

Then he [Jesus] said to them, "Anyone who welcomes
a little child like this on my behalf welcomes me, and
anyone who welcomes me also welcomes my Father
who sent me." (v. 48)

. . .

Jesus loves children. And so do we.

We love them for their delight in starlight and rainbows.

We love them for their collections of seashells and bird feathers.

We love them for their questions—why, how, when and where?

We love them for their answers—because it is, and it is so.

We love them for their misspellings and mispronunciations.

We love them for their finger paintings and clay creations.

We love them for their patience and for their spontaneity.

We love them for their bravery and their boldness.

We love them for their honesty and transparency.

We love them for their innocence and their wisdom.

We love them for their triumphs and their stumbles.

We love them for their love for puppies and kittens and us.

We love children. And so does Jesus.

Dear Jesus, lover of children, watch over and care
for our children today. Shelter them. Feed them.
Keep them from harm. Comfort them. Heal them.
Help them to grow and flourish and
become like you.

POWER IN PRESENCE

The presence of Jesus results in multiple healing miracles.

Matthew 15:21–28
Miracles Happen in the Presence

Mark 7:31–37
Hear Ye! Hear Ye!

Mark 8:22–26
An Eye-Opening Event

John 7, 8
Look Beneath the Surface

John 9
Who's to Blame? Don't Tell Me!

• Matthew 15:21–28 •

*"Dear woman," Jesus said to her, "your faith is great.
Your request is granted." And her daughter was
instantly healed. (v. 28)*

. . .

Miracles happen.

Miracles happen when a parent's unfailing love and a healer's gift combine to restore wholeness to a child's life. We don't talk today so much of demons or demon possession as when Jesus walked the earth. But our children face challenges in growing up that, if not exactly the same as in Bible times, can be equally destructive, even disabling, and difficult to escape.

Risky behaviors, substance abuse, and crippling depression too often accompany the teenage journey from adolescence to adulthood. Each young life compromised, or tragically lost, in this growing-up transition, is one too many. Our children end up on the streets, in trouble of various kinds, in our emergency rooms and our hospital beds with injuries and illnesses, confusion and distress.

What can we do? Where can we go? How can we help our children?

The woman in this story, whose daughter was "severely tormented" refused to give up. She took her plea to the Healer. Even when the Healer seemed reluctant to take her case, she persevered. She had a faith-full response for each apparent objection. And her patience, fortitude, and persistence were honored by the Healer. Her daughter was released from the bonds of illness that held her.

Dear Master Healer, look on our child today with compassion and pour out your love and healing power in a miraculous way. Restore health and vibrancy and peace to this young life. Thank you for your mercy and grace.

• Mark 7:31–37 •

He [Jesus] sighed and said … "Be opened!" Instantly
the man could hear perfectly, and his tongue was
freed so he could speak plainly! (vv. 34–35)

. . .

The healer asks, "What brings you in today? What's the trouble? How can I help you?" But what if the patient can neither hear nor speak? How can she express her concerns and requests? How can she tell her story? How can she make herself understood? I suppose she could try sign language or write on a notepad, despite the related challenges and constraints.

But what if her patient has an advocate, a friend or a family member who knows her well, understands her language, by whatever means communicated, and is capable and willing to translate carefully, accurately, compassionately, so that healer and patient exchange clear and trustworthy information? What a gift! What a blessing! What a contribution to health and healing.

Dear Lord, thank you for friends and family
who care and who give of themselves, their time,
energy, skills, and love to make healing possible.

• Mark 8:22–26 •

Then Jesus placed his hands on the man's eyes again, and his eyes were opened. His sight was completely restored, and he could see everything clearly. (v. 25)

...

Sometimes healing and relief occur quickly, as when a splinter is removed from a finger, or an itchy, allergic reaction responds quickly to appropriate medication, or a sprained ankle resolves within a few hours or days.

But more often, healing is a prolonged process requiring weeks or months to achieve full recovery. Severe injuries may require surgery and intensive care followed by prolonged rehabilitation. Cancer treatment may involve a staged process, including surgical measures, followed by radiation and chemotherapy. Heart disease often involves complex interventional procedures, rehabilitation, and ongoing medical management.

Necessary treatments may be time-consuming, unpleasant, and associated with side effects or complications. Staying the course requires courage, patience, and trust in healers and caregivers. But what a moment for thanksgiving and rejoicing when the course is complete, the body is healed, and new life begins!

Dear Lord, thank you for healing mercies, however difficult and prolonged. Give me courage, patience, and strength to keep moving forward to complete the journey to recovery, health, and wholeness.

• John 7:1–9 •

*Jesus' brothers said to him, "You can't become famous
if you hide like this! If you can do such wonderful
things, show yourself to the world!" (v. 4)*

• • •

Medical science has made great advances over the past two hundred years and is capable of doing many wonderful things today. Antiseptic techniques for surgery came into use in the late 1800s, dramatically reducing the incidence of infection following surgery. Anesthesia, providing for pain-free procedures, was developing about the same time. The 1900s brought advances in medical education and the introduction of antibiotics to treat infectious diseases. The late 1900s and early decades of the twenty-first century have witnessed amazing progress in gene therapies, robotic surgery, and "minimally invasive" surgical techniques. Wonderful things indeed, relieving pain, treating illness, restoring function, promoting health, prolonging life.

---

*Thank you, Lord, for giving knowledge, skill, and
wisdom to medical pioneers whose vision and
courage have advanced the science of medical care
and brought relief, recovery, and
healing to so many.*

• John 7:10–24 •

*"Why should you be angry with me for healing a man
on the Sabbath? Look beneath the surface so you can
judge correctly."* (vv. 23–24)

. . .

Common things are common. Of course, it's true, but it
sounds like nonsense. We speak of the "common cold,"
the "common flu," a "common sprain." They are common
because they occur frequently (commonly), affect many people,
and generally respond to routine (common) measures and
treatments. But what happens when common illnesses fail to
respond to common management? When routine treatments
don't seem to work? When the illness is resistant to standard
therapy?

The best doctors are those who are trained to look beneath
the surface, to consider other possibilities, to go deeper into
a patient's medical history, to review the medical literature, to
consult trusted colleagues, to refer to a specialist for a second
opinion. So, don't be dismayed or discouraged if your doctor
recommends that a consult or second opinion is in order.

---

*Thank you, Lord, for persistent doctors who go
the second mile, probing more deeply, to find the
cause of my condition and get me
on the road to health.*

• John 7:25–53 •

Jesus ... called out, "Yes, you know me, and you know where I come from. But I'm not here on my own. The one who sent me is true, and you don't know him."
(v. 28)

. . .

Sometimes mother knows best. She knows things. She knows her child. She knows when something is out of sync, when her child's appetite is off, when her baby feels feverish, when her child is uncharacteristically irritable, when his skin tone is pale, when he seems listless and tired.

She knows when to withhold solid food and when to push fluids. She knows when it is okay to send her child to school and when to send a note instead. She knows when to allow him to play outdoors and when to insist on rest and sleep. She knows when and how to employ home remedies and when to consult the doctor. Sometimes mother knows best.

She may not have had the benefit of clinical training. She may not be familiar with the latest diagnostic tools or the medication of choice. Call it intuition, or wisdom, or inner knowing, or mother's love. But she knows when she is helping and when she needs help in difficult circumstances.

Thank you, Lord, for mothers and for their precious gift of knowing.

• John 8:1–11 •

*Jesus ... said to the woman, "Where are your
accusers? Didn't even one of them condemn you?"
"No, Lord," she said. And Jesus said, "Neither do I. Go
and sin no more." (vv. 10–11)*

. . .

It's not fair. It's not right. It's not the way my life was meant
to be. I had hopes and dreams of a family, a home, a career.
But things went askew, out of control, sideways with detours
and dead ends that I somehow couldn't avoid. I never thought
I would become what I am today, bought and sold (or rented)
for someone's momentary good time. Sometimes they call
me a companion, or an escort, sometimes the labels are more
common, more coarse, spiteful. It's hard to be so casually used
and dismissed, disrespected, mistreated, even abused.

But today was the worst. To be called out and set up for
open, public ridicule, accused by those who used me and
profited from my body and my skills, then finally, threatened
me with street justice and the most humiliating and painful
punishment. It's too much to bear. I thought it was the end.

Then I heard through the fog of my terror and despair, one
kind and gentle voice, someone speaking calmly to me, to
me—not at me, not about me—but to me, "Where are your
accusers?" I opened my eyes and glanced around. Gone. Every
last one of them had disappeared. "Didn't even one on them
condemn you?" Through a torrent of tears, hands shaking,
between sobs of exquisite relief, "No, Lord." And then Jesus
said, "Neither do I." In that moment, I experienced forgiveness
and healing. What could I do but go and start over—a new
path, a new purpose, a new life.

Dear Lord, you who rescue lost and lonely souls, thank you for your unanticipated mercies, your unexpected grace, your unlimited forgiveness, and your unfailing love. I place my life in your hands today.

• John 8:12–20 •

Jesus … said, "I am the light of the world. If you follow me, you won't have to walk in darkness, because you will have the light that leads to life." (v. 12)

...

Light has healing properties. Researchers around the world are discovering beneficial effects of light on a wide variety of conditions, including chronic pain, depression, migraine headaches, wound healing, and skin conditions such as psoriasis and acne. Different wavelengths of light, from near infrared (NIR) through the spectrum of color to blue light, have been shown to have different applications. Physicians and scientists are working diligently to understand the most effective uses and doses of treatment with light, known as phototherapy. Simple and inexpensive to use, phototherapy, under the guidance and prescription of trained physicians, is achieving growing acceptance in medical science.

Dear Lord Jesus, light of the world, thank you for the healing properties of light. May the light of your healing presence be evident in my life today.

• John 8:21–30 •

Jesus continued ... "Unless you believe that I AM who I claim to be, you will die in your sins." (vv. 23–24)

. . .

Why is it so hard to believe things we don't understand? There are many things about medical care that are hard to understand. It is hard to understand how imaging procedures work—how do X-rays and CT scans and MRIs create pictures of the skeleton and organs inside the body? How do medications work in the body to fight infections, destroy tumors, relieve pain, control blood pressure, make it easier to breathe? How are robots designed to perform delicate surgery under the hands of skilled surgeons?

We don't always understand, but we believe. We believe because others have gone through a similar experience, and we have seen the results. We believe, sometimes, because we are at the end of the rope, desperate for answers, for relief, for healing. We believe, mostly, because we trust the doctor, the nurse, the Healer.

Healing Lord, thank you for the healers who follow in your trail. Help us to trust their training, their knowledge, their experience, their good intent toward us. We may not always understand, but we believe.

• John 8:31–38 •

*Jesus said … "You will know the truth and the truth
will set you free." (vv. 31–32)*

. . .

Some things are hard to hear and harder yet to accept. A
diagnosis of cancer or another debilitating disease with an
uncertain or frightening outcome is difficult to hear. It seems
the mind cannot immediately accept or comprehend the words
spoken, as though the very words are foreign to the ear.

Questions cascade one upon another. How can this be? How
could it have happened to me? What am I going to do now?
How will this change my life? What happens now? Where do I
go from here?

Despite the shock, the questions, the uncertainty, there is
a certain freedom in hearing and understanding the truth.
Now we know. Now we can work with our healers to develop
a course of action. Now we can engage our resources in
responding to the challenge. Now we can think about our
options, plan for the future, and hope for a good outcome.

*Lord God, give me, I pray, ears to hear and a spirit
of understanding. Guide me as I think about the
future, explore my options, and make decisions.
Give to my healers, I pray, wisdom and skill as
they advise me and care for me. Restore my hope
and give me peace.*

• John 8:39–59 •

They replied, "We aren't illegitimate children!
God himself is our true Father." (v. 41)

. . .

The story is told of a young boy who was conceived out of wedlock, and whose father had long ago left him and his mother alone to fend for themselves. The boy and his mother were faithful churchgoers. They admired the pastor and enjoyed the fellowship, but the boy was shy and insecure about his identity. He was worried about how he would be treated by other kids if they knew who he really was. On a particular day, as the worship service ended, the pastor stood at the door, greeting parishioners as they filed out of the church. The boy tried to be as inconspicuous as possible, hoping to slip out without being noticed. He was frightened and embarrassed when the pastor singled him out with a smile and hearty greeting, "Son, I know who you are, and I know your father," he paused, then in a deep and resonant voice, pronounced for everyone to hear, "You are a child of God."

Dear Lord, Father of all, thank you for giving each of us life, for loving us, for never abandoning us, never rejecting us, for having open arms and gentle hands, for putting your arms around us and calling us your children, your own.

• John 9:1–5 •

"Rabbi," his disciples asked him, "why was this man
born blind? Was it because of his own sin or his
parents' sins?" "It was not because of his sins or his
parents' sins," Jesus answered. (vv. 2–3)

• • •

Why? Whose fault is this? Who's to blame?

It's a natural human tendency to look for a culprit, to assign blame, to find fault. Whose fault is it? Whose sin is responsible when something goes wrong—when a baby is born in any way less than perfect, when two cars collide at the corner, when the business fails, when a marriage comes apart at the seams. And the sad truth is, sometimes there is an obvious person who is responsible—when a driver ignores the stop sign, when a business manager steals from the company, when a marriage partner acts in a manner to destroy trust.

But sometimes tragedies occur that are not in our control, that are not the fault of those most affected. Sometimes, at conception, the genes and chromosomes come together in a way that results in lifelong disability. Sometimes a young person, in the bloom of life, contracts cancer. Sometimes a crippling injury occurs during an athletic contest. Sometimes otherwise healthy people are struck by debilitating diseases— multiple sclerosis, dementia, heart disease—and it's nobody's fault.

That's what Jesus said. He said that neither the blind man nor his parents sinned. Sometimes bad things happen. No one is at fault, and God does not abandon us. He still hears our prayers, and despite whatever outcome, God loves us and does not assign blame to us.

Dear Lord, when we don't know why, and we don't understand how, we pray for a sense of your presence and for evidence of your love. Give us trust in you, hope for the future, and peace for today.

• John 9:6–7 •

Then he [Jesus] spit on the ground, made mud with the saliva, and spread the mud over the blind man's eyes.... The man went and washed and came back seeing! (vv. 6–7)

...

It is known that the lining of the mouth, or oral mucosa, heals from minor injury more quickly than external skin. Researchers who have studied this phenomenon have discovered that human saliva contains factors, including protein, enzymes, and microscopic white blood cells, that fight infection and promote healing. So, does "licking a wound" really help a minor cut or injury heal more quickly? Experts urge caution, since human saliva may also contain harmful bacteria that can cause infection. However, there remains the possibility that scientists may someday have the ability to isolate and manufacture the healing elements of saliva in a safe and sterile environment for use in medical treatment of skin injuries. It seems that the more we learn about our bodies, the more there is to know. Sometimes bad things happen. No one is at fault, and God does not abandon us. He still hears our prayers, and despite whatever outcome, God loves us and does not assign blame to us.

Creator God, thank you for building into our bodies healing properties that protect, defend, and restore us when we are fighting illness and injury.

• John 9:8–25 •

*The man replied. "But I know this: I was blind, and
now I can see." (v. 25)*

. . .

There's an old saying, "the proof is in the pudding." In other
words, the outcome is evidence that the process works.
It's another way of saying that while we don't know exactly
how healing happens, we know that a broken bone has knit
back together, that new skin has covered a "skinned knee," that
the abdominal pain has resolved. Sometimes, when we we're
not sure how, when there's no satisfactory explanation, we're
tempted to call it a miracle. And maybe, just maybe, miracle is
the best explanation of all.

---

*Lord God of the miraculous, thank you for
ordinary miracles—headache goes away, nausea
and dizziness resolve, minor cuts and bruises heal.
And thank you for the unexpected, unpredictable,
unexplainable miracles that demonstrate your
mercy and love in ways beyond knowing.*

• John 9:26–41 •

*"If you were blind, you wouldn't be guilty," Jesus
replied. "But you remain guilty because you claim
you can see." (v. 41)*

. . .

Please, don't tell me. I don't want to know. I just can't handle
it right now.

It's easy to understand how bad news on top of bad news can
become almost too much to bear. The temptation to ignore or
deny troubling symptoms is an all-too-common response to
illness. If I don't acknowledge it, don't talk about it, maybe it
will just go away. Maybe it will; maybe it won't. But the truth is
that if an illness can be diagnosed early in its course, and can be
treated promptly and appropriately, there is a better chance of a
good outcome.

---

*Dear Lord, help me to recognize and acknowledge
my own human frailty and my tendency to
overlook worrisome symptoms. Help me be willing
to seek help. Give me the courage to hear hard
truths, and the willingness to yield to the art and
science of healing. Restore me, I pray. Trusting in
your love and care.*

SECTION IV

THE LORD IS MY SHEPHERD

Hope and promise are found in
The Lord's Prayer and Psalm 23.

Luke 10, 11
The Lord's Prayer

Luke 12, 13
Don't Worry!

Luke 14, 15, 16
Humility in a Gown

John 10, 11, 12
The Lord Is My Shepherd

Luke 17, 18
Thank You, Lord

• Luke 10:1–20 •

"Whenever you enter someone's house, first say, 'May God's peace be on this house.'" (v. 5)

• • •

Illness and injury are disruptive to a family. The daily routine changes when a member of the family is struggling with a serious health challenge—perhaps bedridden, unable to work or go to school, unable to contribute to the welfare of the home, unable to carry out ordinary daily duties, or perhaps even isolated or hospitalized.

In addition to experiencing fear, anxiety, and worry, the family must figure out how to care for their loved one who is ill, and how to fill in the gaps, how to care for themselves and each other. It is a stressful time for all. Personal responsibilities, priorities, and schedules must adapt. There may be financial challenges. It may be hard to find time for relaxation, recreation, rest, and sleep.

In these stressful circumstances, the Healer says, "May God's peace be on this house."

Dear Lord, in this time of unusual difficulty and stress for our family, we pray, first, for your healing grace to be poured out on our loved one who is ill, for healing and health and strength. We pray, too, for ourselves and for our family, each one facing personal challenges in coping with this illness that has struck a person we love. We ask your blessing, that "God's peace may be on this house."

115

• Luke 10:21–24 •

Jesus … said, "O Father, Lord of heaven and earth,
thank you for hiding these things from those who
think themselves wise and clever, and for revealing
them to the childlike." (v. 21)

. . .

Wisdom does not require university education or advanced academic degrees. Wisdom is more commonly acquired by quiet observation of life around us. Wisdom may emanate from unexpected sources—the very young or the very old. Wisdom is patient and thoughtful and reserved. Wisdom does not necessarily equate with fame or prosperity. Wisdom can be easily missed in the noise of everyday life. Wisdom does not shout from the pulpit or the grand stage. It is more likely to speak softly, even whisper. Wisdom is not in a hurry. It is more likely to walk slowly or to sit patiently. Wisdom may be more readily found in the musty word of ancient sages than in the latest, hot-off-the-press, best seller.

Dear Lord, source of all wisdom, be in my
mind and heart today. Help me to listen and
understand. Give me wisdom to know your will
and your way for my life.

• Luke 10:25–35 •

"When he saw the man, he felt compassion for him.
Going over to him, the Samaritan soothed his wounds
with olive oil and wine and bandaged them. Then he
put the man on his own donkey and took him to an
inn where he took care of him." (vv. 33–34)

...

He was not the first to happen on the scene, but he was the first to stop and help. I doubt that he was an emergency medical technician (EMT), but perhaps he had treated injuries in the past. He didn't have much in the way of equipment or supplies, but he did the best he could with what he had on hand. He soothed the injured man's wounds with oil and wine and bandaged them. That regimen remains good first-aid treatment today. Alcohol cleanses and disinfects. Oil soothes and heals. Bandages control bleeding and protect raw wounds from further injury and contamination.

He didn't stop there. He put the man on his donkey and took him to shelter, watching his patient over the night and arranging for ongoing care before continuing his journey the next morning. Perhaps he was an EMT, or an angel in disguise, or maybe he was just a good neighbor.

Dear Lord, I'm not a doctor, a nurse, or an emergency medical technician. But I can be a good neighbor. Make me willing to serve those in need.

• Luke 10:36–37 •

*"Now which of these three would you say was a
neighbor to the man who was attacked by bandits?"
Jesus asked. The man replied, "The one who showed
him mercy." (vv. 36–37)*

. . .

Who is my neighbor?

Maybe it's the couple who live next door on the other side of the fence, house hidden by the hedge. We don't see them often. Occasionally, we chat briefly when they take their dog for a walk. Their children are grown and gone from home. And we don't have much in common.

Or maybe it's the folks with whom we share an office. Grandparents we call; those with whom we share stories and photos. We have aging parents who require attention, and we are beginning to experience chronic aches and pains ourselves. At least it's something to talk about over morning coffee.

Or maybe my neighbor is the family quarantined with Covid, unable to leave the house, even to buy groceries, for the next ten days. Or the family whose home was flooded and blown away, utterly destroyed, by the latest hurricane coming ashore yesterday. Or the retired couple whose home burned to the ground in the fires on the west coast.

---

*Dear Lord, help me to recognize and care for my
neighbor. Soften my heart. Open my purse strings.
May I be willing to be inconvenienced by the
loss, pain, and sorrow of my neighbor. Give me a
merciful and generous heart, I pray.*

• Luke 10:38–42 •

But the Lord said to her, "My dear Martha, you are
worried and upset over all these details! There is only
one thing worth being concerned about. Mary has
discovered it, and it will not be taken away from her."
(vv. 41–42)

. . .

First things first. Get your priorities straight. No slacking. There's a lot to be done.

That's one way to look at it. Get better. Get up. Get back on your feet. Get back home. Get back to work.

First things first. Sometimes the routine is turned upside down. Sometimes priorities must be reassessed. Sometimes rest and sleep are more important than work. Sometimes walking is more beneficial than running, and chicken soup more nourishing than steak and potatoes.

Lord, help me put first things first. Give me the
strength to relax, release, and recover.
Refresh my body and soul.

• Luke 11:1–4 •

One of his disciples came to him and said, "Lord,
teach us to pray." Jesus said, "This is how you
should pray." (vv. 1–2)

. . .

When Jesus' disciples asked him to teach them to pray, he responded, "When you pray, say,

---

Our Father in heaven,
Hallowed be Your name.
Your kingdom come.
Your will be done
On earth as it is in heaven.
Give us day by day our daily bread.
And forgive us our sins,
For we also forgive everyone who is indebted to us.
And do not lead us into temptation,
But deliver us from the evil one."
Luke 11:2–4 (NKJV)

Matthew's version of this prayer is recorded in the middle of Jesus' famous Sermon on the Mount. It is a bit longer than that of Luke and, in some versions, includes a closing line—"For yours is the kingdom and the power and the glory forever"— that many scholars believe was added later by a copier or translator of the Scriptures.

"Our Father in heaven,
Hallowed be Your name.
Your kingdom come.
Your will be done
On earth as it is in heaven.
Give us this day our daily bread.
And forgive us our debts,
As we forgive our debtors.
And do not lead us into temptation,
But deliver us from the evil one.
For Yours is the kingdom and the power
and the glory forever. Amen."
Matthew 6:9–13 (NKJV)

Regardless of whose version is technically correct, The Lord's Prayer has become one of the best known and most loved passages of Scripture. It is often intoned communally in worship, and as part of memorable ceremonies, such as weddings and memorial services. It is also an essential component of daily devotions for many devout believers. This brief and simple, personal and profound, expression of worship, dependence, petition and praise is as pertinent and precious today as it was two thousand years ago when Jesus first taught it to his disciples.

• Luke 11:5–13 •

"And so I [Jesus] tell you, keep on asking ... keep on seeking ... keep on knocking." (v. 9)

. . .

Sometimes it seems as though my prayers go no higher than the ceiling of the room. Sometimes it seems as though, despite my deep need and fervent request, no one is listening. No one seems to care. There is no apparent answer or response. It seems as though I am alone in my pain and confusion.

It's hard to keep on asking. It seems foolish to keep on seeking and impertinent to keep on knocking when the door remains closed. But Jesus says to do just that—keep on. Keep on asking. Keep on seeking. Keep on knocking. He follows with a promise, "Everyone who asks, receives. Everyone who seeks, finds. And to everyone who knocks, the door will be opened" (Luke 11:9–10).

The answer may not be the one that is anticipated. The way it shows up may be a surprise, and the door that opens may lead to an unexpected place. But God's promise is sure; his love is everlasting, and I am safe within his plan for me.

Dear Lord, give me a sense of your presence; give me confidence in your care for me, and the assurance of your constant love.

• Luke 11:14–28 •

[Jesus] said, "Any kingdom divided by civil war is doomed. A family splintered by feuding will fall apart." (v. 17)

. . .

Illness hurts. It separates and divides. It is accompanied by serious stress—anxiety, worry, fear. It disrupts our lives, our homes, our work, our daily routines. It raises often unanswerable questions—will I get well? How long will this last? Who can I trust? Will I ever be my old self again? How long will the money hold out?

These stresses, and others, often bring great pressure to bear on family relationships. How do we make important decisions? Who decides? How do we resolve differences in opinion? Why is it so difficult to agree? These are not new questions. These questions were being asked in the time of Jesus, and long before. They are as old as the history of mankind. These questions are not unique. They know no geographic or ethnic or religious or political boundaries. They are human questions. They are asked, discussed, debated, confronted, sometimes resolved (and sometimes not) in the surgery waiting room, outside the ICU, at home while awaiting test results.

Jesus said that civil war destroys a kingdom, and "a family splintered by feuding will fall apart."

Dear Lord, we pray that you will hold our family in the palm of your hand. Keep us together as we walk through this storm. Help us to think clearly and to make wise decisions. Anoint our words with compassion. Strengthen the bonds of love that hold us together.

• Luke 11:29–36 •

"Your eye is like a lamp that provides light for your body. When your eye is healthy, your whole body is filled with light." (v. 34)

. . .

God's first words recorded in Scripture constitute a command, "Let there be light." It follows that there was light, and it was good. Jesus describes the eye as a lamp illuminating the body. When our perspective, our view of life and the world around us, is characterized by wonder, delight, hope, and optimism, it is as though our bodies are filled with health-imparting light. We are more resilient, better able to withstand illness, better equipped to recover quickly when assaulted by disease or injury.

Lord God, Light-Giver, send someone to open the blinds so that I can see the light, read again the get-well cards from family and friends, watch for encouraging words from my caregivers, and let God's healing light enter my body and soul.

• Luke 11:37–54 •

*"So clean the inside [of the cup] by giving gifts to the
poor, and you will be clean all over." (v. 41)*

. . .

How many are poor? How many are hungry? How many
are homeless? How many are uneducated? How many
are abused? How many are broken? How many are friendless?
How many are lonely? How many are neglected? How many are
overlooked? How many are passed by? How many are unseen
and unheard? How many are ill? How many have little hope?

---

*Dear Lord, give me a heart of sensitivity,
generosity, and compassion for all of these.*

• Luke 12:1–12 •

"The very hairs on your head are all numbered.
So don't be afraid.... " (v. 7)

. . .

Today, the population of the world is approaching eight billion people. Together, China and India make up about a third of earth's human inhabitants. The United States accounts for only about 5 percent of the world's population.[7] So many people, so many names, so many mouths to feed, so many languages, so many differing customs and religions.

How does God keep us all straight? Yet Scripture assures us that he does. God knows us all by name. We are all his much-loved children. He knows our hopes and dreams and our cares and concerns.

Father, God of all peoples on earth, hear the
prayers of your children today and answer
according to your mercy, grace, and compassion.

• Luke 12:13–21 •

*Jesus replied … "yes, a person is a fool to store up
earthly wealth but not have a rich relationship
with God." (vv. 14, 21)*

. . .

It's a sad truth. There's no way to sugarcoat it or soft pedal
it. We all die. There is an inevitable end to our existence on
earth. Some of us will live as long as a hundred years. Some
of us will only take a few breaths following birth. The average
lifespan in the United States for men is about seventy-five years,
a few more for women.[8] That may seem like a long time when
viewed from our teens, not so long when we retire from work.

So, what do we do? How do we manage our lives? How do
we prepare for the end of life, whenever it may come? We value
our life, care for our body, treat our illnesses and injuries, love
and care for our families, treasure and enjoy our friendships, be
kindhearted and generous toward those less fortunate, prepare
for the future, and trust God for the outcome, whenever and
however that may come.

---

*Dear God, Lord of life, time, and eternity, make of
my life what you would have it be. Strengthen me
in life, comfort me as death approaches, and keep
me eternally in your love.*

• Luke 12:22–34 •

Jesus said.... "I tell you not to worry about everyday life—whether you have enough food to eat or enough clothes to wear. For life is more than food, and your body more than clothing." (vv. 22–23)

. . .

"Don't worry. Be happy." Bobby McFerrin's catchy tune became a huge hit in 1988–89, and it remains popular today.[9] The sentiment echoed in McFerrin's song is reminiscent of the admonition of Jesus, "Don't worry." Observe the birds—God feeds them. Look at the colorful flowers—God clothes them. So don't worry. God loves you and will provide for you. Place your trust in him.

Dear Provider God, take away my doubts, fears, and worries. I place my trust and hope in you.

• Luke 12:35–48 •

"You also must be ready all the time, for the Son of Man will come when least expected." (v. 40)

. . .

Get ready for school. Get ready for work. Get ready for church.

Get ready for the party. Get ready for the in-laws. Get ready for exams. Get ready for surgery. Get ready to go home. It seems as though we're always getting ready for something, and then it's done. Then we're getting ready for the next thing, the next deadline, the next event.

Jesus encourages us to "be ready," to maintain a sense of readiness for whatever may come. Being ready means being aware, following the routine, looking after the little things, managing daily tasks. Being ready may not be exciting, may not draw attention, may not elicit praise. But when things begin to fall apart, when the accident happens, when illness strikes, being ready shows up and makes a difference.

Dear Lord, help me be ready today and every day for both the routine and the unexpected. Thank you for giving me wisdom, courage, and strength sufficient for today.

• Luke 12:49–59 •

"Families will be split apart...." (v. 52)

. . .

Stress accompanies illness. It is inevitable that we experience uncertainty and distress when faced with troubling symptoms that we do not understand. We are torn between hope and despair, between dependence and independence, between the differing opinions of family and caregivers. Emotions run high; sometimes there are sharp words, and sometimes there are tears. Always there are questions; some that go unanswered, and some with unwelcome answers.

God of all comfort, be in this room today. Be in my life today. Be with my family today. Be with my caregivers—my doctors and my nurses— today. Heal my wounds. Heal our strained and fractured relationships. Give us peace for today.

• Luke 13:1–5 •

*"Do you think those Galileans were worse sinners
than all the other people from Galilee?" Jesus asked.
"Is that why they suffered? Not at all!"* (vv. 2–3)

. . .

Let's face it. We've all messed up at one time or another. We've all made mistakes in life. We've all done things for which we feel shame and regret. We wish it were not so. We wish we could take it all back and start over. But there it is. And sometimes we're tempted to think that our aches and pains and illnesses are just punishment for our past sins and mistakes. Not so, says Jesus the Healer, not at all. That is not why we suffer.

---

*Jesus, Lord of repentance and recovery, teach me
to stop carrying a heavy burden of sadness and
guilt. Don't allow the failures of my past to take
away my hope for the future. Heal me, I pray, in
body and soul.*

• Luke 13:6–9 •

The gardener answered, "Sir, give it one more chance.... If we get figs next year, fine. If not, then you can cut it down." (vv. 8–9)

• • •

Have you ever wanted one more chance? One more opportunity to say, "I'm sorry." To give one more hug. To whisper, "I love you." To do the dishes, take out the trash, make the bed, wash the car? To send a card, buy a bouquet, take a photo, bake a cake? To go to the kids' soccer game, band concert, school play? One more chance to take a walk, watch an old movie, read a book, write a poem? One more chance to be who you really are, who God created you to be? Start today. Make a list and check one thing off today, another tomorrow, and another again the next day.

Lord God of second chances, make of my life today what you would have it to be.

• Luke 13:10–17 •

One Sabbath day as Jesus was teaching in a
synagogue, he saw a woman who had been crippled
… for eighteen years…. Jesus called her over …
touched her, and instantly she could stand straight.
(vv. 10–13)

. . .

Sunday. Monday. Tuesday, Wednesday. Thursday. Friday.
Saturday.

I don't know what day it is that you are reading this. I
don't know what ailment you are experiencing. I don't know
what tests have been completed or what procedures are
being considered. But I know this—every day is a good day
to experience God's healing grace. Illness and injury take no
holiday nor vacation. That's why hospitals, emergency rooms,
and clinics are open twenty-four hours a day, seven days a
week. That's why first responders are always prepared to deal
with accidents and disasters, why nurses work around the
clock every night and day, why doctors are on call twenty-four
seven—to be there when you need us, and by the grace of God,
to contribute to your healing. May you have a blessed day today.

Lord God of time and eternity, thank you for
round-the-clock healthcare and for doctors and
nurses who are always on call for emergencies and
unexpected illnesses and accidents. May I express
my gratitude to someone for caring for me today.

• Luke 13:18–30 •

"And people will come from all over the world—from east and west, north and south" [Jesus said,] *"to take their places in the Kingdom of God."* (v. 29)

. . .

Where are you from? What is your home country? Where did you grow up? These are important medical questions. Some diseases are more commonly found in different countries, different nationalities, and different ethnic groups. One's cultural background and family history may be essential information when investigating the origin and cause of a particular illness.

But wherever your origin and whatever your background— from all over the world, east and west, north and south—you will be cared for. We will do our best to make you comfortable, to keep you safe, to keep you informed, to make it easy for you, to help you back to health. That's our commitment to you today.

Creator God, Father of all humanity, thank you for your boundless love, your constant care, and your infinite mercy. Be my Healer today.

• Luke 13:31–35 •

Jesus replied, "I will keep on casting out demons and healing people today and tomorrow." (v. 32)

. . .

It's been two weeks since I underwent cataract surgery on my right eye, and next week I'll undergo the same surgery on my left eye.

My right eye is healing beautifully. I can see better today than I could when I was eight years old. I am using eyedrops each day to prevent infection and reduce inflammation. It doesn't happen overnight, but slowly, steadily, hour by hour, and day by day, healing is taking place. Maybe that's why we're called patients—healing requires patience.

Thanks be to God for doctors and artificial lenses and operative lasers and antibiotic drops. Thanks be to God for new vision.

• Luke 14:1–14 •

He [Jesus] gave them this advice: "When you are invited to a wedding feast, don't sit in the seat of honor.... Instead, take the lowest place at the foot of the table." (vv. 7–8, 10)

. . .

Admission to the hospital is a humbling experience. First come the questions—important, essential questions—but personal and sometimes embarrassing. Why are you here today? Where does it hurt? How long has it been going on? Sensitive questions about "unmentionable" things. Then you're asked to remove your clothing and put on a hospital gown, big enough to go around you twice, but not designed to cover you entirely. Finally comes the examination—listening, pushing, prodding—nothing hidden from the trained eye of your clinician. Your food is brought to you on a tray. Your medicines are delivered on a schedule. You can't even get out of bed or go to the restroom without assistance. It's an exercise in humility. We understand. It's all important, all for a good purpose, to find out what's wrong and set about to fix it. But it's humbling, nevertheless.

Dear Lord, take away my pride and self-sufficiency. May I be as your trusting child, willing to be humbled, willing to be seen and known and touched by your healing care.

• Luke 14:15–24 •

"But they all began making excuses." (v. 18)

...

Excuses, excuses.

I know, I know, I need to see a doctor. The pain in my hip has been bothering me for weeks. It's getting worse, not better, but I'm too busy to get it checked out.

Or how about this one? Yes, the doctor said I should take the medicine three times a day for ten full days, but it's only been four days and I'm feeling a lot better. I don't think I need to take any more of those nasty pills.

Or maybe it goes like this. That odd-looking sore on my foot just won't seem to heal. It's not particularly painful and no one can see it with my socks on, so what's the point in going to the clinic?

No more excuses. None. Don't ignore the signs and symptoms of disease. Don't overlook the doctor's counsel and directions. Listen, treat as directed, and follow up.

---

*God of truth, make of me an honest witness today.
Give me the courage to communicate openly,
the wisdom to understand the process, and the
patience to comply with my treatment plan for my
wellbeing and for your glory.*

• Luke 14:25–35 •

"But don't begin until you count the cost." (v. 28)

. . .

What will this cost? That's a good question to ask. There's no doubt about it—medical care is expensive. Prescriptions are expensive. Procedures are expensive. Hospital care and nursing home care carry large price tags. Insurance helps, but it doesn't cover everything all the time. It's important to plan ahead and count the cost. But some things can't be valued in financial terms, in dollars and cents alone.

What is the value of a newborn baby's smile?

How much is an extra year of life worth?

Can a price tag be placed on a pain-free holiday at home with family?

What would one pay for a long, limp-free walk in the park?

How much is it worth to hear the voice of a songbird for the first time?

What are the words, "Your cancer is in remission" worth?

Dear Lord, help me to count the cost, to comprehend the true value of healing. Help me to fully appreciate life and health and strength, the ability to think and do. Thank you for the inestimable gifts of health, healing, and hope.

• Luke 15:1–7 •

"Rejoice with me because I have found my lost sheep."
(v. 6)

. . .

H ave you ever wandered away from the crowd and gotten stuck in a scary place?

Perhaps you have a sense of how that lonely lost sheep felt, separated from the flock, frightened, stuck in a dense thicket with no idea how to get to shelter. Illness can do that. It can separate us from family and friends, isolate us, confine us to bed, or worse yet, to a room with no visitation allowed. So, the misery of serious illness is made harder to bear by isolation and loneliness, without the presence and comfort of loved ones. We try to make the best of a difficult situation through the healing presence of caring nurses, staff, and spiritual caregivers along with virtual contact with family and friends.

Dear Lord and Shepherd of the lonely, bring your healing presence into this room today. Surround this bed with your love and grace and give us peace.

• Luke 15:8–10 •

"Rejoice with me for I have found my lost coin." (v. 9)

* * *

Have you ever lost something that you greatly valued? Maybe it was your reading glasses, or your car keys, or your billfold. Or maybe it was something of sentimental value, an old family photo, your wedding ring, or your high school yearbook. It could have been something essential for your family's wellbeing—money for the week's groceries, or fuel for your car, or the house payment. And I'm sure you looked in all the likely places—the bedroom dresser, the kitchen cabinets, the glove compartment in the car. And when it was found, there was relief and joy and celebration.

---

*Thank you, Lord, for being the
finder of lost things.*

• Luke 15:11–32 •

*"This son of mine was dead and has now returned to
life. He was lost, but now he is found."
So the party began. (v. 24)*

. . .

Family relationships can be difficult, especially when important issues are being confronted. Who is responsible for making decisions when someone is sick or disabled? Who will look after the family business? How do we relate to a returning brother or sister who has been estranged from the family for a long time? How do we work out sensitive issues when someone insists on having their own way? How do we get past questionable decisions and unfortunate history? It can be very hard to patch things up and move ahead. Sometimes it's helpful to involve a professional counselor or a trusted pastor or chaplain to help sort things out and find a way through. Sometimes it means saying, "I'm sorry. Please forgive me." Sometimes it means forgiving, forgetting, and together forging a new future.

---

*Dear God of new beginnings, forgive us our debts
as we forgive our debtors. Lead us to a place of
love and reconciliation, we pray.*

• Luke 16:1–18 •

Jesus [said] to his disciples ... "Use your worldly resources to benefit others and make friends. Then, when your possessions are gone, they will welcome you to an eternal home." (vv. 1, 9)

...

It's a wonderful thing to have lots of friends, and more wonderful yet to have really good friends. Friends are great to have around for celebrations—holidays, birthdays, weddings—happy times together. But they're even more appreciated when things go bad, when life takes an unfortunate turn, when illness or misfortune strikes. A card or call from a caring friend may not change the circumstances at all, but somehow it seems more manageable, more bearable, when a true friend says, "I'm here for you. I'm praying for you. I care." Whether these words come to you via greeting card, phone call, text message, or in person, the day seems better, your problems less burdensome.

Lord of love and caring, help me to nurture and grow good friendships in the good times, telling my friends how much I love and appreciate them, in full confidence that they'll be there for me when times are tough.

• Luke 16:19–31 •

"If they won't listen to Moses and the prophets, they won't be persuaded even if someone rises from the dead." (v. 31)

. . .

It's hard to change my mind. I'm just set in my ways. I've always done it this way and I'm not about to change now. Don't even try to convince me. I don't care about someone's so-called expert opinion. Just take my word for it.

Or maybe there's another way. Maybe times have changed for the better. Maybe there's new technology that will help me. Maybe I should listen more closely to my doctor and my nurse and my family. Maybe if I change my mind and change my ways, I'll feel better and recover more quickly.

Dear Lord, give me an open mind, a willing heart, and a new life. Thank you for hearing my prayer.

• John 10:1–16 •

*Jesus said, "I am the good shepherd; I know my own
sheep, and they know me." (v. 14)*

. . .

The relationship between a shepherd and the sheep is a close and intimate one. A shepherd lives with the sheep twenty-four hours a day. The shepherd knows the sheep and the sheep recognize the voice of the shepherd. The shepherd leads the sheep to pasture and water, protects them from predators, and watches them closely for signs of illness or injury, treating their wounds and symptoms. The shepherd helps the ewes deliver and care for their lambs. Those who care for us, our parents, teachers, pastors, friends, doctors, and nurses, are our shepherds. We place our trust in them. Jesus is the Good Shepherd, who knows us best and loves us most. We can take our worries, fears, and burdens to him. He hears and cares.

Dear Lord and Shepherd of the sheep, thank you for your abiding presence in my life. Thank you for providing my every need, for protecting me from danger, seen and unseen. I pray that you will walk with me now through this difficult time. Care for me. Comfort and encourage me. I place my trust in your goodness and mercy for now and forever.

Psalm 23
The Shepherd Psalm
The Lord is my shepherd;
I have all that I need.
He lets me rest in green meadows;
he leads me beside peaceful streams.
He renews my strength.
He guides me along right paths,
bringing honor to his name.
Even when I walk
through the darkest valley,
I will not be afraid,
for you are close beside me.
Your rod and your staff
protect and comfort me.
You prepare a feast for me
in the presence of my enemies.
You honor me by anointing my head with oil.
My cup overflows with blessings.
Surely your goodness and unfailing love will
pursue me all the days of my life,
and I will live in the house of the Lord forever.

• John 10:17–30 •

*Jesus replied, "The proof is the work I do in my
Father's name.... The Father and I are one."*
(vv. 25,30)

. . .

The name of one's father is important. Men carry the names
of their fathers from generation to generation. Women
customarily carry the name of their father until marriage and
sometimes choose to keep it for a lifetime. A father's name
conveys identity, heritage, and legacy. Family attributes and
abilities, knowledge and skills often reappear in successive
generations for decades or even centuries. Sometimes illness
and infirmity, not infrequently identified with a long-ago
father's name, are genetically transmitted along family lines.

---

*Dear Lord and Father of humankind, may I bear
your name with grace, gratitude, and humility.
Thank you for caring for me as a loving father
cares for his children. I place my life in
your hands today.*

• John 10:31–42 •

*Jesus replied ... "Don't believe me unless I carry out
my Father's work. But if I do his work, believe in the
evidence of the miraculous works I have done."*
(vv. 37–38)

• • •

Good health is important. When health breaks down, the
gifts of a healer are sought to assist in recovery. But how
can we tell if healing claims are legitimate? How can we have
confidence in the healer? How can we trust that the procedure
is likely to have a positive outcome? We can talk with others
who have had a similar experience. We can seek a second
professional opinion, or we can take a chance and hope for the
best. It's been said that "what you see is what you get." Don't
expect something different from or better than what you have
learned. Jesus said of his healing work, "believe in the evidence."
Two thousand years later, that's still good advice.

---

*Lord God, give me the knowledge to understand,
the wisdom to assess and evaluate, and the
courage to make an appropriate healing decision.*

• John 11:1–16 •

Then he [Jesus] said, "Our friend Lazarus has fallen asleep, but now I will go and wake him up." … They thought Jesus meant Lazarus was simply sleeping, but Jesus meant Lazarus had died. (vv. 11, 13)

* * *

Sleep is usually a good thing. Adequate sleep is necessary for healthy, vibrant living. For most adults, this means an average of seven to eight hours of sleep each night (or day). Too little sleep, or too much, can suggest an underlying health problem. When illness or injury strikes, more sleep is required to allow the body to direct its resources toward the healing process. Medically induced sleep (anesthesia) is essential for potentially painful procedures and surgery. The very deep sleep that we refer to as "coma" is often associated with brain injury and other serious illnesses. Jesus referred to the death of his friend, Lazarus, as sleep.

God who never sleeps, teach me to pray with the innocence of a little child: "Now I lay me down to sleep; I pray the Lord my soul to keep. If I should die before I wake, I pray the Lord my soul to take."

That's a good "go to sleep" prayer for all of us.

• John 11:17–29 •

Jesus told her [Martha], "I am the resurrection and the life. Anyone who believes in me will live, even after dying. Everyone who lives in me and believes in me will never ever die." (vv. 25–26)

...

Sooner or later we all die. That is the inescapable outcome of human existence. We value life with all its pleasures and cares even as we acknowledge life's inevitable ending in death. In verse 25 of this devotional Scripture reading, Jesus told the sister of Lazarus, "I am the resurrection and the life. Anyone who believes in me will live, even after dying."

That's an amazing, incredible, beyond-understanding promise. We have all experienced the death of a loved one, the memorial service, the burial or scattering of ashes. Who has witnessed a resurrection? And who would believe their story? Nevertheless, we believe Jesus' promise to be reliable and true. We believe that we will live again.

Dear Lord, in the face of death and dying, give us the calm assurance of your life-giving power and hope of eternal life to come.

• John 11:30–44 •

*Then Jesus shouted, "Lazarus, come out!" And the
dead man came out, his hands and feet bound in
graveclothes, his face wrapped in a headcloth. Jesus
told them, "Unwrap him and let him go." (vv. 43–44)*

. . .

Just imagine.

Imagine graves opening all over the world. Imagine those
drowned in the deep emerging from the water. Imagine those
burned in fire, those missing in war, those lost in wilderness
and desert returning to life. Imagine reunion of parent and
child, husband and wife, lifelong friends and comrades, family
reunions of untold generations.

Just imagine.

Jesus said, "Lazarus, come out!" And Lazarus heard the voice
of Jesus and came out, released from the darkness of the tomb
and the bonds of death.

Believers accept the story of Lazarus as real and true, and we
believe that Jesus will say those words again someday, and we
will all hear, and live and breathe and love again—forever.

---

*Dear Lord, thank you for life, real life,
now and everlasting.*

• John 11:45–57 •

They said to each other, "What do you think? He won't come for Passover, will he?" (v. 56)

. . .

Should I undergo surgery or not?

- Should I take the flu vaccine or not?
- Should I see the doctor or just tough it out?
- Should I buckle up for just a short ride around the block?
- Should I take vitamins and supplements every day?
- Should I eat less and exercise more?

Yes. No. Maybe. How do I know? Which expert do I trust?

Opinions differ. Circumstances differ. People have different priorities and different needs at different times of life.

Dear Lord, help me to make good decisions, health-promoting, life-giving decisions and give me the courage and good sense to carry out my intentions.

• John 12:1–11 •

*A dinner was prepared in Jesus' honor. Martha served,
and Lazarus ... ate with him. Then Mary took ...
expensive perfume ... and she anointed Jesus' feet.*
(vv. 2–3)

• • •

Healthcare is a twenty-four seven endeavor. Twenty-four hours a day, seven days a week, three hundred and sixty-five days a year, healthcare professionals are at work, or on-call as needed, in hospitals and clinics around the world. That includes holidays, such as Christmas and New Year's Day, and special community and family events. After all, disasters happen at random; accidents don't telegraph their occurrence; new babies make their appearance at all hours of day and night. Nurses, doctors, lab technicians, housekeepers, dietary staff, and many others willingly devote their time to care for us when needed. Today is a good day to personally thank our caregivers for their charity and devotion to our recovery and wellbeing.

---

*Dear Lord, may I be grateful for the little things,
the mundane duties, the everyday comforts
provided by my caregivers. May the fragrance of
my thankfulness cheer them and bless them
in their tasks.*

• John 12:12–36 •

Many in the crowd had seen Jesus ... raising him
[Lazarus] from the dead, and they were telling others
about it. That was why so many went out to meet
him—because they had heard about this
miraculous sign. (vv. 17–18)

. . .

One day it's in the headlines. The next day it's commonplace. And by the next day, it's forgotten. The twenty-first century is only two decades gone, and already we have witnessed the mapping of the human genome, startling (and controversial) advances in stem cell research, and the widespread adoption of minimally invasive and robotic surgery. Along the way, cigarette smoking has become less and less pervasive, and deaths from heart disease have decreased dramatically. Tomorrow will bring more change and better therapies, but we should be grateful for past advances, even as we benefit from current capabilities, and look toward the future with anticipation and hope.

Thank you, God, for brilliant researchers and
far-sighted scientists and innovative practitioners
whose diligence, creativity, and persistence have so
blessed our lives.

• John 12:37–50 •

Jesus shouted to the crowds, "If you trust me, you are trusting not only me, but also God who sent me. For when you see me, you are seeing the one who sent me."
(vv. 44–45)

. . .

Among us there are those who see things as they are, some who desire to see but cannot, and some who choose not to see despite the evidence. It's always been that way. And there are consequences for deliberately ignoring the evidence. Cigarette smoking contributes to tens of thousands of deaths from heart and lung disease each year. Failure to wear seatbelts causes more severe injuries and more frequent deaths in the event of an accident. Failure to wear life jackets results in drownings that could have been avoided. Alcohol and substance abuse contribute to thousands of deaths annually. And that's the sad truth.

Dear Lord, open our eyes that we may see clearly, understand deeply, and act wisely to save lives and live fully.

• Luke 17:1–10 •

"When you obey me you should say, 'We are
unworthy servants who have simply done our duty.'"
(v. 10)

...

Regardless of one's position or job description, there are many unpleasant tasks that must be performed in a clinic or hospital—dirty tasks, smelly tasks, tedious tasks. Someone must collect samples of blood and other body fluids for analysis in the laboratory. Someone must clean open wounds and change bandages. Another must cause someone discomfort by examining, probing, invading the body with needles or other instruments. Someone must clean patient rooms, operating rooms, and bathrooms making them sterile and safe. Others must wash thousands to trays and dishes and cooking utensils. Every day they go about their duties calmly, quietly, without complaint, making their contribution to safety and quality care for all of us. And if asked, they would say, "We have only done our duty."

Dear Lord, thank you for those who care for us
with diligence and compassion.

• Luke 17:11–19 •

Jesus asked, "Didn't I heal ten men? Where are the other nine? Has no one returned to give glory to God except this foreigner?" (vv. 17–18)

. . .

Leprosy is an old and most cruel disease. Leprosy results in bodily deformity, as the loss of feeling in fingers, toes, nose, and ears allows injuries to go unnoticed and untreated, culminating in disability and loss of essential function. For centuries, lacking effective treatment and fearing the disease would spread to others in the family and community, lepers have been forcibly separated from society, banned from the community, and torn from their families. Lacking the opportunity to earn a living, lepers have lived on the fringes—poor, hungry, ragged, outcast.

Of ten lepers healed by Jesus, only one returned to express his gratitude. We can only imagine what might have kept the other nine from thanking their Healer. Perhaps:

- One hurried directly home to embrace his spouse and surprise his children.
- Another went straight to his former place of business to put things in order.
- A third had an outstanding warrant for his arrest and made good his escape.
- A hope-filled fourth stopped by the home of his former betrothed.

And so it went. The future couldn't begin soon enough as they returned to life as they once knew it—healthy, hearty, hopeful—and, unfortunately, forgetful of the One who was responsible for their healing and restoration.

Thank you, God, for your healing mercy in my life. Thank you for those who care for me today. Thank you for their knowledge and skill. Prompt me to express my heartfelt gratitude today and every day.

• Luke 17:20–37 •

Jesus replied ... "For as the lightning flashes and lights up the sky from one end to the other, so it will be on the day when the Son of Man comes." (vv. 20, 24)

...

"I never saw it coming."

"It just happened out of the blue."

"One day I was fine—the next I'm flat on my back."

"How could this happen so suddenly?"

Jesus said that's the way life is. People are eating and drinking, marrying, and giving in marriage, buying and selling, planting and building. Then disaster strikes—suddenly, without warning, no time to prepare, no means of escape. Earthquake, tornado, flood, pandemic disease.

We do the best we can. We pitch in and help each other. We restore and rebuild.

Lord God, Creator of the universe, in you we place our ultimate hope and trust, for today and tomorrow, because you love and care for us.

• Luke 18:1–8 •

*One day Jesus told his disciples a story to show that
they must always pray and never give up.... "But
when the Son of Man returns, how many will he find
on the earth who have faith?" (vv. 1, 8)*

. . .

I believe in prayer. I have prayed since I was a little child. I
believe that God hears my prayers. I believe that prayer makes
a difference. But I'm having a hard time understanding why
my prayers just don't seem to be getting through. This illness
has interrupted my life, disrupted my plans, and challenged
my faith. It's confusing. I'm worried and afraid. Where is God?
Does God hear me? Does God care? How long must I wait?

Jesus taught his disciples to keep on praying. Despite your
illness, despite your inability to see a way forward, despite your
anxiety and fear—keep on praying. God hears. God knows.
God understands. God will answer. Perhaps not immediately;
perhaps not in a way that you might expect, but God will
answer. Keep on praying. You are safe in God's hands.

---

*God of my past, my present, and my future, I pray
today that you will give me confidence to trust
your will and your way in my life.*

• Luke 18:9–17 •

Then Jesus told this story. "Two men went to the
Temple to pray...I tell you, this sinner, not the
Pharisee, returned home justified before God."
(vv. 9, 10, 14)

. . .

Illness is an "equal opportunity," or perhaps better stated, an "equal importunity" experience.

- The president of the company has a bicycle accident.
- A woman in the homeless shelter has an abscessed tooth.
- A flu epidemic goes through the nursing home.
- A contaminated food product causes digestive distress in the local high school.

All are vulnerable, and all experience accidents and maladies of various sorts in the course of a lifetime. Uninterrupted health and wellness are neither to be expected nor experienced.

Father of all, rich or poor, weak or powerful,
young or old—we praise you for the good times,
depend upon you in the hard times,
entrust our future to you, and care
for each other along the way.

• Luke 18:31–34 •

*Taking the twelve disciples aside, Jesus said … "The
Son of Man … will be mocked, treated shamefully,
and spit upon. They will flog him with a whip and kill
him, but on the third day he will rise again."*
(vv. 31–33)

. . .

It's a hard thing, perhaps life's hardest thing, to experience
a portent of death. We understand the inherent deadly risk
of war. We accept the mortal danger of firefighting and risky
rescue attempts. We accommodate a sentence of death in our
legal system.

But when the doctor says you have only a short time to
live, it's another matter. It's real. It's personal. It's serious and
shattering. Everything changes—plans, priorities, hopes, and
desires. What may have seemed essential yesterday is no longer
important, and what seemed trivial becomes immediately
critical.

Jesus knew his time was short. He knew that his last hours
would be painful and his death certain. But he knew something
else that made all the difference—he knew his death would be
but a temporary interruption of his life—that he would live
again. And because that's just what happened, those who believe
in him will live again too.

---

*Precious Lord of life, I believe. Thank you for the
living hope of resurrection to life eternal.*

162

• Luke 18:18–30 •

He [Jesus] replied, "What is impossible for people is possible with God. (v. 27)

. . .

Who is a good person? Easy answer—don't lie, cheat, steal, kill, or dishonor your parents. But Jesus was never one for easy answers. More often, he answered a question with another question, "Why do you call me good?"; or with a story, such as, A certain man did this or that; or with an extravagant, even impossible, demand, "Sell everything you have and give to the poor."

Then he provides a solution, "What is impossible with you is possible with God."

Whatever seems impossible to me today is always possible with the God of yesterday, today, and tomorrow.

Dear Lord, be the answer to my questions, the solution to my problems, my comfort in difficulty, and my hope for the future.

• Luke 18:35–43 •

A blind beggar was sitting beside the road.... He begun shouting, "Jesus, Son of David, have mercy on me!" ... And Jesus said, "All right, receive your sight! Your faith has healed you." Instantly the man could see. (vv. 35, 38, 42–43)

. . .

Don't be afraid to ask.

Some may say it's foolish, or it's a bother, or nobody cares, or it's not worth the effort. Don't be dismayed or discouraged. This Scripture reading tells us to ask anyway. The blind man asked, "Jesus, Son of David, have mercy on me!" Those in charge tried to shut him up, but he wouldn't be silenced, "Son of David, have mercy on me." When Jesus stopped and asked, "What do you want?", he answered, "Lord, I want to see." And the blind man, the doggedly persistent man who refused to be discouraged or hushed, immediately received his sight. Don't be afraid to ask again and again.

Gracious Healer, like the blind man who wouldn't stop asking, I come to you again today praying for your healing mercy. Listen to my prayer. Answer in your wisdom and your love. Give me the grace to accept with praise and thanksgiving.

COMFORT IN CRISIS

Jesus demonstrates love, joy, and peace despite betrayal, denial, death.

Luke 19, 20, 21
Plague and Pandemic

Luke 22 and John 13
Heartache, Betrayal, Denial

John 14, 15, 16
Love, Joy, Peace, and Healing

John 17, 18, 19 and Luke 22
The Healer and Me

John 19 and Luke 23
Death and Grieving

• Luke 19:1–10 •

So he [Zacchaeus] ran ahead and climbed a sycamore-fig tree beside the road.... When Jesus came by, he looked up at Zacchaeus and called him by name. "Zacchaeus!" he said. "Quick, come down! I must be a guest in your home today." (vv. 4–5)

. . .

Have you ever been all alone ... up a tree ... out on a limb ... hanging on for dear life ... hoping against hope that the limb won't break and send you tumbling to the ground? Have you ever felt lonely in a crowd ... people happy, laughing, talking, and joking ... but you were reluctant ... too anxious, too frightened, to join the fun? Have you ever heard someone say, "Come down from that difficult place. I want to spend some time with you, get to know you better, relieve your distress, restore your joy"? Perhaps then you know how Zacchaeus felt when Jesus called him down from the tree in the presence of the crowd and invited himself to dinner at the home of Zacchaeus. Jesus came to seek and save those who are lost, and he comes to you today as he did to Zacchaeus and invites you to spend time with him.

Dear Savior of those who are out on a limb, I gladly accept your invitation today. May I be firmly grounded in your presence.

• Luke 19:11–27 •

A nobleman was called away.... Before he left, he called together ten of his servants and divided among them ten pounds of silver, saying, "Invest this for me while I am gone." (vv. 12–13)

...

The human body is, according to the psalmist, "fearfully and wonderfully made" (Ps. 139:14, NKJV). From conception to gestation to birth, our bodies are formed and come into being. Our hearts beat thousands of times each day without prompting. We breathe in and breathe out without a conscious thought. We taste, chew, and swallow our food, triggering an automatic digestive and metabolic process that turns corn and beans and apples into muscle and bone and energy. Our eyes behold beauty. Our ears transmit melody. Our nostrils detect fragrance and aroma. Our tongues appreciate flavor, and our skin thrills to the touch of a loved one. Our hands paint and sculpt and build; our legs and feet propel us across valleys and up mountain peaks. Our brains coordinate and orchestrate it all through millions of electrical impulses that course along complicated communication networks throughout the body.

It is our responsibility to care for our marvelous and "wonderfully made" bodies, keeping ourselves healthy and productive, and developing our God-given skills, talents, and abilities for the benefit of the world and our fellow human beings. Our investment of time and energy in our health, through good nutrition, regular rest and exercise, building positive relationships, making good choices, and thanking God for our blessings, pays rich dividends in experiencing a whole life.

Dear Lord, thank you for life and breath and strength, for the ability to think and to do. Bless me as I seek to make the most of your marvelous gift of being alive.

• Luke 19:28–48 •

As he [Jesus] rode along … his followers began to
shout and sing … "Blessings on the King who comes
in the name of the Lord!" … But as he came closer to
Jerusalem and saw the city ahead, he
began to weep. (vv. 36–38, 41)

. . .

Perhaps you recall the television sports show, *Wide World of Sports*, that appeared on ABC TV from 1961 to 1998. The show's standard intro, "the thrill of victory and the agony of defeat," became a popular part of American vernacular for many years. It seems to me that this simple phrase caught on mostly because we all understand it at a deep and personal level. We have all experienced the joy and excitement of victory, whether it was winning the class spelling bee, hitting a homerun at the sandlot softball game, being asked to the high school prom, or landing that first job. And we have all endured the agony of defeat—straggling in last in the charity 5K run, watching the cake fall flat in the baking contest, missing out on a hoped-for promotion, acknowledging the end of a serious relationship.

When the parade is over, and the crowd has dispersed, when the cheers are silenced, and the confetti is being swept off the street, it may be hard to recall the thrill of victory, however exhilarating it may have been. Likewise, the feelings of disappointment and regret associated with a loss, however crushing, may be alleviated with time.

God cares about you, not so much about your wins and losses, as about you, personally. You can go to him with your ups and downs, your hopes and dreams, your desires and needs. He hears and he cares.

Dear Lord, thank you for loving me just as I am.

• Luke 20:1–8 •

They demanded, "By what authority are you doing all these things? Who gave you the right?" (v. 2)

. . .

Who writes the orders?
Who dispenses the medication?
Who cleans and stitches the wound?
Who pushes the wheelchair?
Who cooks the food?
Who delivers the tray?
Who cleans the room?
Who keeps the records?
Who interprets the test?
Who keeps me safe?
Who comforts and prays with me?

There are many caregivers who are committed to your health and wholeness. Each one is trained and committed to your safety and your recovery.

Thank you, Lord, for each one who cares for me today. I pray that you will be the caregiver to each and every one of them as they go about their important tasks.

• Luke 20:9–19 •

Jesus looked at them and said, "Then what does this Scripture mean? 'The stone that the builders rejected has now become the cornerstone.'" (v. 17)

. . .

Rejection is important, even critical, when its purpose is to detect and correct mistakes, to remove imperfections, to control contamination, to eliminate dangerous variability, to advise against unnecessary or inappropriate treatment.

But rejection is wrong when it excludes people, when it discriminates on the basis of race, color, creed, nationality, gender, age, social status, or any of a host of identifiers that have nothing to do with personhood, capacity, ability, or values.

Lord God, Creator of all, we are all your children. Help us to love each other, care for each other, and honor each other as brothers and sisters in God's family.

• Luke 20:20–47 •

*"Beware of [those who] ... love to receive respectful
greetings as they walk in the marketplaces.... Yet they
shamelessly cheat widows out of their property."*
(vv. 46–47)

. . .

The organization and financing of modern medical care is
complex. Many nations have some form of government
sponsored health care for all. Others rely on a free market
approach with multiple players in the market, including
government at many levels, private insurance companies, and
varying levels of personal responsibility. No system is perfect.
Each has advantages and disadvantages.

How can we be sure that no one is placed at risk or left out,
that everyone has access to necessary care at an affordable
cost? It's a complex question that has challenged generations of
leaders and governments around the world.

---

*Dear Lord of us all, bless those who work to
provide healthcare in an equitable manner.
Bless those who care for the poor, the homeless,
the helpless, the widow, the orphan, and the
immigrant. Bless those who seek to find solutions
to thorny problems of access and funding. Give us
wisdom, conviction, love, and compassion that
none may be left out, that all may be served.*

• Luke 21:1–4 •

"I tell you the truth," Jesus said, "this poor widow has given more than all the rest." (v. 3)

. . .

Hospitals and clinics in the United States are organized for business in four basic ways. Some are funded and managed by government entities—city, county, state, and federal hospitals, of which the Veterans Administration and hospitals such as Los Angeles County and Cook County (Chicago) are notable examples. The investor-owned, for-profit sector accounts for about 18 percent of all hospitals, including Hospital Corporation of America (HCA), Community Health Systems (CHS), Tenet, and others. Not-for-profit community hospitals comprise about half of all United States hospitals, of which faith-based hospitals are a significant component.[10]

Charitable contributions are an important funding source for tax-exempt (not-for-profit) hospitals, enabling expansion and enhancement of facilities and equipment, supporting research and development of advances in diagnosis and treatment, and providing care for patients with special needs or lack of resources. Every contribution is important, from the smallest to the largest. While single, large donations often result in greater publicity and recognition, it is the many smaller donations that demonstrate widespread community support for the organization. These contributions, large and small, are essential to the ongoing ability of the organization to provide quality care for everyone in need.

Dear Lord, give us generous hearts to ensure access to safe and quality healthcare for each and all who come to us seeking relief, comfort, and healing.

• Luke 21:5–38 •

He [Jesus] added, "Nation will go to war against
nation.... There will be great earthquakes, and there
will be famines and plagues in many lands." (v. 10)

. . .

New Year's Day, 2020, heralded a year of promise, as governments, businesses, communities, and families made plans. Little did we know that within three short months our daily lives would be radically changed, our world turned upside down, our priorities and plans altered in ways we could not have predicted. The Covid-19 virus spread around the world like a universal tsunami, attacking in successive waves of disease and death, each larger and more devastating than its predecessor.

Words and phrases infrequently used became part of the common vernacular—pandemic, quarantine, isolation, personal protective equipment. Churches, schools, and office buildings emptied as we transferred education, work, and worship to home. Meetings went virtual; handwashing, social distancing, and face masks became customary. Not since the Great Depression and the Second World War had the entire world experienced a disaster of this magnitude and duration.

Jesus told his followers not to be surprised when wars, earthquakes, famines, plagues, and disruptions of the natural order occur. He didn't predict or promise carefree, prosperous, or healthy lives. He encouraged his followers (and us) to pray for courage and the ability to stand and speak out for God and truth and right. "Pray," he said, "that you might be strong enough to escape these coming horrors" (Luke 21:36).

Dear Lord, we thank you for your words that prepare us to face this day's challenge. Give us strength for today, we pray, and courage and compassion to care for each other. In your name.

• Luke 22:1–13 •

Jesus sent Peter and John ahead and said, "Go and prepare the Passover meal, so we can eat it together."
(v. 8)

. . .

Advance preparation is essential to any important venture. An airplane flight is preceded by a checklist of weather, fuel, and instruments. An ocean cruise requires adequate food, supplies and staff to last several days on the open sea. The construction of a building is dependent on detailed drawings, essential materials and skilled craftsmen working in sequence to deliver a project on time.

A surgical procedure is no different. A safe and effective outcome is the result of a carefully planned combination of people, processes, equipment, and supplies coming together. Highly trained professionals—surgeons, anesthesiologists, nurses, technicians, and staff make sure the room and necessary instruments are clean, sterile, and appropriately organized. The systems of lighting and temperature, medications and fluids, computers, surgical robots, and imaging equipment are functioning properly. A pre-operative checklist is observed— the right patient, the right procedure, the right location, the right time.

Dear Lord, be with me this day as I undergo this healing procedure. Thank you for the preparation that has made this possible—the education, training, and skill of my caregivers; the sophisticated technology that enables the work, and the careful processes that contribute to a successful outcome. Now I place myself in your hands, asking your blessing upon us all this day.

• John 13:1–17 •

*So he [Jesus] got up from the table, took off his robe,
wrapped a towel around his waist, and poured water
in a basin. Then he began to wash the disciples' feet,
drying them with the towel he had around him."*
(vv. 4–5)

. . .

In the time of Jesus, upon entering a house, it was customary for people to wash their feet after walking dusty streets and roads wearing sandals. It was also customary to carefully wash their hands before each meal. Cleanliness is important in the prevention and transmission of infectious disease. Frequent handwashing is the single most effective measure to avoid passing bacterial and viral illnesses to others.

Lord Jesus, Healer, make us sensitive to the little things that prevent disease and promote healing— clean air, clean water, clean surfaces, and, most of all, clean hands. Teach us to eat healthfully, to exercise prudently, to value our relationships, to think positively, and to trust in your providence.

• Luke 22:14–20 •

Jesus said, "I have been very eager to eat this Passover meal with you." (v. 15)

. . .

Good nutrition is essential to the healing process. A balanced diet provides adequate protein for growth and repair of injured tissues; sufficient carbohydrates to supply the daily energy needs of the body, and healthy fat sources to store energy, nutrients, and hormones. A balanced diet also supplies vitamins and minerals to facilitate normal metabolic processes.

Creator and Healer, give me the knowledge and commitment to care for my body, keeping myself well-nourished so that I may live life to the fullest, avoiding disease and functioning each day at my best.

• Luke 22:21–38 and John 13:18–38 •

"But here at this table, sitting among us as a friend, is the man who will betray me." (Luke 22:21)
"I tell you the truth, Peter—before the rooster crows tomorrow morning, you will deny three times that you even know me." (John 13:38)

. . .

Someone has betrayed your trust, turned their back on you, maligned your character, gossiped about you, lied about you, cheated you out of what was properly yours, all the while smiling and acting as though they were your friend.

Someone has denied knowing you, has acted as though they never met you, wouldn't be seen with you in public, wouldn't admit to any serious relationship with you, all the while walking with you and sharing your table.

Betrayal hurts. Denial hurts.

If you had known before, before all this happened, would you have chosen them for friends? Would you have allowed them into your inner circle … trusted them with your money? Would you have nurtured their friendship? Knowing what you know now, what will you do? Will you give up on them, ignore them, chastise them, throw them under the bus, report them to the church, charge them with a crime? Or will you forgive them, seek to restore them, give them another chance?

Dear Lord, Healer of relationships, you have given me another chance many times. I pray for a forgiving spirit and for a loving heart.

• John 14:1–14 •

Thomas said, "We have no idea where you are going,
so how can we know the way? Jesus told him, "I am
the way, the truth, and the life." (vv. 5–6)

. . .

Have you ever been homeless? Tossed about from place to place, living in a makeshift shelter on a vacant lot? Entire wardrobe consisting of the worn-out clothes on your back? Not sure where your next meal will come from? Or how you will make it through the winter, or even the next month?

How would you feel if someone you knew as a child, someone you trusted and admired, offered you a chance to get back on your feet in a better place, in a real home, with heat and air conditioning, carpeted floors, hot and cold running water, an indoor bathroom, and three meals a day? And instead of offering you a map with directions to this place, your old friend simply tells you to throw your bag in the trunk and jump in the car for a free ride?

Can you believe it?

Would you accept or reject that invitation? Jesus said that his Father's house has many rooms, with one prepared just for you.

Dear Lord Jesus, I accept your invitation to a new
life in your big house. Please show me the way.

• John 14:15–31 •

Jesus said, "I am leaving you with a gift—peace of mind and heart. And the peace I give is a gift the world cannot give. So don't be troubled or afraid."
(v. 27)

. . .

Do you have a sense of peace today?

Illness is frightening. Is it a heart attack? Is it cancer? Could it be a stroke? What about pneumonia? When will the tests come back? How bad is it? What can be done? Will it be painful? How can I afford it? How much time do I have?

This is only the beginning of questions, decisions to be pondered, arrangements to be made—all in the midst of fear, anxiety, worry, even depression. It's stressful for patients, families, friends, and associates. All want to know, and too commonly, the answers are unclear, uncertain, consisting of probabilities, "most common" possibilities, "best guesses," contingent on a range of variables.

How does one cope? How does one relax? How does one rest and sleep at night? Who does one trust?

Dear Lord Jesus, Healer, I look to you now for peace of mind and heart as I face this illness. Take away my fear and give me a sense of your presence and peace.

185

• John 15:1–17 •

*"I have told you these things so that you will be filled
with my joy. Yes, your joy will overflow!"* (v. 11)

. . .

Do you have a source of joy in your life?
Joy that is deeper than a sense of excitement or
exhilaration, more durable than momentary pleasure? Do you
have an abiding sense of joy that sustains you through times
of sadness and difficulty? Real joy is like a deep spring of clear,
cool water within you from which you can draw as needed to
refresh your soul. Joy that is always there, always available; joy
that never runs dry despite the circumstances surrounding your
life. That's what Jesus promises.

Do you have someone who loves and cares for you? Someone
upon whom you can depend in good times and bad? Someone
who cares for you despite an occasional disagreement or
misunderstanding? Someone who loves you when others have
abandoned you? Are you that someone for someone who
needs your love? Love is essential to rich relationships and an
abundant life. Love is so important that in John 15:17, Jesus
referred to it as a new commandment: "This is my command:
Love each other."

---

*Dear Lord, source of love, joy, and peace, be as a
well of living water for me today. May I embrace
your command to love, experience the joy of your
presence in my life, and rest in the peace
of your promises.*

• John 15:18–27 •

"Since they persecuted me, naturally they will persecute you. And if they had listened to me, they would listen to you." (v. 20)

. . .

Illness is bad enough without having to experience conflict and dissension at the same time. But that's often the way it is when we are stressed to manage an illness while going on with the challenges of daily life. Doctors express differing opinions about the proper course of action. Caregivers have different ways of delivering quality care. Family members are struggling to handle additional responsibilities and help make difficult decisions. We become fatigued and our emotions are frayed.

Dear Lord, heal our relationships today. Pour healing salve over our raw emotions. Give rest to those of us who are weary. Give us the ability to see our way through. Build bridges to bring us together in this difficult time.

• John 16:1–15 •

*"When the Spirit of truth comes, he will guide you
into all truth." (v. 13)*

. . .

Truth is often hard. Hard to speak. Hard to hear. Hard to
comprehend, assimilate, accept. But it is necessary. Despite
commonly held misperceptions, most of us prefer to know
the truth about our illness, treatment options, and prospects
for the future. It is neither kind nor prudent for truth to be
withheld from those most directly affected by it. Truth should
be shared with a gentle spirit of honesty and compassion,
accompanied by hope as reasonable and warranted.

---

*Dear Lord, we pray that you send your Spirit of
Truth to enlighten us today. Give us ears to hear
the truth, hearts to accept the truth, and spirits to
bear the truth with courage and fortitude.*

• John 16:16–33 •

"You will weep and mourn ... but your grief will suddenly turn to wonderful joy." (v. 20)

. . .

Grief is often the companion of hard times. Grief over what once was, over what has been lost, over what could have been. Regret surfaces. Apologies are shared. Tears are shed. Jesus promised his followers, "You will grieve, but your grief will suddenly turn to wonderful joy.... Ask, using my name, and you will receive, and you will have abundant joy" (John 16: 20, 24).

Dear Lord, comfort and sustain us in our grief and restore us to your joy.

• John 17:1–25 •

*After saying all these things, Jesus looked up to heaven
and said, "Father, the hour has come.... I am praying
not only for these disciples but also for all who will
ever believe in me through their message." (vv. 1, 20)*

. . .

To the young, life seems almost endless. Grandparents
have lived forever; their stories of old times seem ancient,
mythological even. To those of middle age, there comes a
grudging awareness of a distant horizon to life's journey, to be
acknowledged, if not entirely accepted. To the elderly, who have
lost dear friends and family to the grave, the imminence of one's
own death becomes a stark reality for which to be prepared.

As Jesus celebrated his last Passover with his disciples and
pondered the nearness of his own death, his thoughts and
prayers were for his followers, those who had walked and talked
with him, those who shared his sorrows and joys. As he prayed
for them, he assured them of the reality of life to come, eternal
life to follow the end of earthly existence. And he revealed to
them the way to eternal life through a living, vibrant knowledge
of the one true God and Jesus himself, sent to earth to live with
them for a while.

---

*Dear Lord of Life, today I claim your promise of
eternal life. Lead me to know and love you and to
trust your living Word.*

• Luke 22:39–46 •

[Jesus] knelt down and prayed, "Father, if you are willing, please take this cup of suffering away from me. Yet I want your will to be done, not mine."
(vv. 41–42)

. . .

Why me? Why this illness? Why now? I don't understand. There's no understanding it—no apparent cause. Yet here I am in a hospital bed unable to walk ten steps without assistance. Worried about what the future holds, waiting for answers, hoping for the best.

Dear Lord Jesus, I pray your prayer from the garden. If you will, take away my suffering, but if not, then your will be done.

John 18:1–19:16 and Luke 22:47–23:25 •

Now with blazing torches, lanterns, and weapons,
they [Roman soldiers] arrived at the olive grove. He
[Jesus] stepped forward to meet them. "Who are you
looking for?" he asked. "Jesus the Nazarene," they
replied. "I AM he," Jesus said. (John 18:3–5)

. . .

Perhaps you've been betrayed by someone you loved. So was Jesus.

Perhaps you've been arrested by the authorities. So was Jesus.

Perhaps you've been abandoned and denied by close friends. So was Jesus.

Perhaps you've been tried and convicted on false charges. So was Jesus.

Perhaps you've been rejected by your church and community. So was Jesus.

And when a fight broke out and his enemy was injured, Jesus healed him on the spot, no questions asked, no accusations made, no hesitation.

Dear Lord Jesus, forgive those who've hurt me;
heal their pain and be my strength in trouble.

• John 19:16–37 and Luke 23:26–49 •

They took Jesus away ... nailed him to the cross ...
and Pilate posted a sign on the cross that read, "Jesus
of Nazareth, the King of the Jews" ... so that many
people could read it. (John 19:16–20)

...

"Father, forgive them, for they don't know what they're doing." (Luke 23:34)

"Dear woman, here is your son." To John: "Here is your mother." (John 19:26–27)

To a dying thief: "Today, you will be with me in paradise." (Luke 23:43)

"My God, my God, why have you abandoned me?" (Matthew 27:46/Mark 15:34)

"I am thirsty." (John 19:28)

"It is finished!" (John 19:30)

"Father, I entrust my spirit into your hands!" (Luke 23:46)

Forgiveness. Love. Compassion. Abandonment. Suffering. Resignation. Trust.

Dear Lord Jesus, when my time comes, may my
"seven last words" echo yours.

• John 19:38–42 and Luke 23:50–56 •

They wrapped Jesus' body with the spices in long sheets of linen cloth ... and since the tomb was close at hand, they laid Jesus there. (John 19:40, 42)

...

There was no family visitation, no flowers, no memorial ceremony, no funeral processional. The body of Jesus was taken from the place of execution to a nearby garden tomb where it was wrapped in linen cloth and perfumed spices. Then those who had cared for him went home to observe the Passover Sabbath. That holy day must have been a most sad and fearful day after the tragic events of Friday. No one guessed, no one anticipated what the sunrise of the first day of the week would bring.

Dear Lord of Sabbath, give us rest following tragedy and death. Give us time to grieve and mourn, to relax and sleep, to reflect and ponder, to lean upon each other, to share our stories, to imagine a different future. Give us the gift of your presence in our time of sorrow.

NEW LIFE

Praise for life anew and the promise
of life everlasting.

John 20 and Luke 24
Hallelujah! The Healer Lives!

John 21
When the End Is Not the End

• John 20:1–10 and Luke 24:1–12 •

"Why are you looking among the dead for someone who is alive? He isn't here! He is risen from the dead!"
(Luke 24:5–6)

...

Astounding! Incomprehensible! Unbelievable!

It wasn't for lack of prior knowledge. Jesus had told his followers what to expect, but somehow it never got beyond their ears. Now his body was gone, and they couldn't believe their eyes. "He is risen," they were told, but his followers still seemed to have ear trouble. How could it be so?

But it was so! The garden tomb could not hold Jesus. He had risen to live again. And because he lives, we will live again too. The grave is powerless to hold those who die believing this story to be true, those who trust in the One who rose that early morning.

Lord God of life restored, all praise to your name. Hallelujah! Jesus lives! Hallelujah! He is the giver of life to all who believe. Hallelujah!

• John 20:11–21:24 and Luke 24:13–49 •

"Why are you frightened?" he [Jesus] asked. "Why
are your hearts filled with doubt? Look at my hands.
Look at my feet. You can see that it is really me. Touch
me and make sure that I am not a ghost." ... As he
spoke, he showed them his hands and his feet.
(Luke 24:38–40)

. . .

Testimonies to the appearance of Jesus following his resurrection are found in all four gospels and in Paul's letter to the Corinthians. If seeing is believing, then these eyewitness experiences provide compelling evidence of Jesus' resurrection:

- To Mary (and a second Mary) in the garden outside the tomb (John 20:14-18).
- To fearful disciples meeting behind locked doors, he brings peace (John 20:19-23).
- To Thomas who doubted, now exclaiming, "My Lord and my God!" (John 20:26-29).
- To disciples on a mountain in Galilee (Matt. 28:16-20).
- To disciples fishing at Galilee, including Peter, forgiven and accepted (John 21:1-14).
- To Cleopas and a friend on the road to Emmaus (Luke 24:13-35).
- To over five hundred witnesses at one time, and to James (1 Cor. 15:6–7).

Dear Lord of the resurrection, through the eyes of faith, we know that we will someday live forever in an earth made new along with those whom we've loved and lost, rejoicing in your presence for eternity.

• Luke 24:50–53 •

Then Jesus led them to Bethany, and lifting his hands
to heaven, he blessed them. While he was blessing
them, he left them and was taken up to heaven.
(vv. 50–51)

. . .

His mission completed, his work on earth accomplished, Jesus returns to his Father in heaven. But his followers are not left alone. Jesus promised to send his Spirit, advocate and comforter, to be with his followers down through the ages, sharing his love, joy, and peace until he returns to take us all to be with him throughout eternity, life without end.

Lord of life, thank you for your love. Thank you for your promise. Thank you for your presence in my life, now and forever.

• John 20:30 to John 21:25 •

*The disciples saw Jesus do many other miraculous
signs in addition to the ones recorded in this book.
But these are written so that you may continue to
believe that Jesus is the Messiah, the Son of God,
and that by believing in him you will have life by the
power of his name.* (John 20:30–31)
*Jesus also did many other things. If they were all
written down, I suppose the whole world could not
contain the books that would be written.* (John 21:25)

. . .

We come to the end of the gospel story of Jesus the Healer,
arguably the best known and most loved story in the
history of our world. But it's not really the end of the story of
Jesus the Healer. His story is an infinite one, not bound to some
thirty years' existence on this earth, rather a story beginning in
eternity past and extending through eternity future. Jesus lives
today in a timeless place beyond our knowing. But he continues
to heal through the hearts and hands of our caregivers. And he
lives within us, healing us—body, mind, and soul.

---

*Dear Lord Jesus, thank you for knowing us, for
hearing us, for loving us, for healing us, for being
by our bedside, for being in our hearts. May we
experience your healing presence
in our lives today.*

Acknowledgments

I want to thank the thousands of people whose lives have touched mine in the practice of medicine over the past half-century—patients, families, and friends who have entrusted your care, and the care of your loved ones, to me. Thank you for your confidence, understanding, and friendship.

I must also express gratitude for the knowledge, skills, compassion, and dedication of our caregivers, modern-day healers—the healthcare professionals who care for us, whether young or old, rich or poor, conscious of their contributions or not, all of us, with our illnesses and injuries.

This book would not have been possible without the thoughtful, inspired work of two storytellers of ancient times, the physician Luke, and the disciple John. Luke and John recorded, each in his own words, complementary stories of the short but world-changing life and career of the Healer.

The original idea for this book, to apply Scriptural stories to modern-day medicine, germinated about a decade ago in conversations with Todd Chobotar, now director of AdventHealth Publishing. It lay dormant for a time as careers and competing priorities took precedence. Todd continues to be a trusted friend and counselor regarding all things "bookish."

The support, professionalism, courtesy, and counsel of the team at HigherLife Publishing nurtured this work from a rough manuscript to a completed book. David Welday saw promise in a sample and provided helpful direction. Michelle Williamson did double duty as project manager and manuscript editor. Her expertise, patience, and gentle guidance made the work of revising, correcting, and polishing a pleasure.

A special thank you to reviewers of the manuscript for your kind, perceptive, and thoughtful comments, many of which appear at the beginning of the book.

Finally, thank you from the depths of my heart to my wife, Jackie, a constant source of energy, encouragement, and enthusiasm, along with our wonderful family, friends, and "family at work" who have contributed in countless ways, large and small, to this project.

Healing Miracle Index

#	Miracle	Primary Source	Secondary Source	Page
1	The Nobleman's Son	John 4:43-54		42
2	The Invalid at Bethesda	John 5:1-15		43
3	A Demoniac in the Synagogue	Luke 4:31-37	Mark 1:21-28	55
4	Peter's Mother-in-law	Luke 4:38-41	Mark 1:29-31	56
5	The First Leper	Luke 5:12-16	Mark 1:40-45	58
6	Paralytic Lowered through Roof	Luke 5:17-26	Mark 2:1-12	59
7	The Man with a Withered Hand	Luke 6:1-11	Mark 3:1-6	62
8	The Centurion's Servant	Luke 7:1-10		69
9	Two Blind Men	Matthew 9:27-31		70
10	A Dumb Demoniac	Matthew 9:32-34		70
11	The Widow's Son at Nain	Luke 7:11-17		71-72
12	The Demoniacs of Gadara	Luke 8:26-39	Mark 5:1-20	81-82
13	The Invalid Woman	Luke 8:40-56	Mark 5:25-34	83-84
14	Jairus' Daughter	Luke 8:40-56	Mark 5:22-43	83-84

#	Miracle	Primary Source	Secondary Source	Page
15	The Demon-Possessed Boy	Luke 9:37-43	Mark 9:14-29	89-90
16	Syrophoenician Woman's Daughter	Matthew 15:21-28		95-96
17	The Deaf-Mute of Decapolis	Mark 7:31-37		97
18	The Blind Man near Bethsaida	Mark 8:22-26		98
19	The Man Born Blind	John 9:1-41		108-110
20	A Blind and Dumb Demoniac	Luke 11:14-32	Matthew 12:22-32	123-124
21	The Crippled Woman	Luke 13:10-17		134
22	The Man with Dropsy	Luke 14:1-4		137
23	The Raising of Lazarus	John 11:1-45		151
24	The Ten Lepers	Luke 17:11-19		157-158
25	Blind Bartimaeus	Luke 18:35-43	Mark 10:46-52	164
26	Malchus' Ear	Luke 22:50-51		192

References to Non-specific Healing Miracles:
- Matthew 4:23-24; 9:35; 12:15; 14:14, 35, 36; 15:30, 31
- Mark 1:32-34; 6:5
- Luke 4:40
- John 6:2

Theme Index

Endnotes

1. Michas, Frederic. "Total number of hospital outpatient visits in the US from 1965–2018," Health Pharma & Medtech/ Health Professionals and Hospitals, July 2, 2020. Retrieved from statista.com.

2. FY 2019 AHA (American Hospital Association) Annual Survey Database. Retrieved from https://www.aha.org/statistics/fast-facts-us-hospitals.

3. "Names." Retrieved from https://www.names.org/lists/most-popular/all-time/#:~:text=Boy%20Names%20%20%20%20Rank%20%20,%20%201905%20%2080%20more%20rows%20. September, 20, 2021.

4. "Population" WorldoMeter. Retrieved from https://www.worldometers.info/world-population/.

5. Ibid.

6. Claypool, John. *Tracks of a Fellow Struggler: Living and Growing through Grief* (Insight Press, New Orleans, 1995).

7. "Population," WorldoMeter. Retrieved from https://www.worldometers.info/world-population/.

8. Arias, Elizabeth PhD et al. "Provisional Life Expectancy Estimates for January through June, 2020," NVSS Vital Statistics Rapid Release, Report 010, February 2021. Retrieved from cdc.gov.

9. McFerrin, Bobby. "Don't worry. Be happy." From the album *Simple Pleasures*, 1988.

10. Fast Facts on US Hospitals, 2021. AHA (American Hospital Association). Retrieved from aha.org.